MADE FOR
MAHARAJAS

MADE FOR
MAHARAJAS

A DESIGN DIARY OF PRINCELY INDIA

BY

AMIN JAFFER

CONSULTING EDITOR

MARTAND SINGH

PHOTO RESEARCH & EDITING

PRIYA KAPOOR

NEW
HOLLAND

This edition first published in 2006 by
New Holland Publishers (UK) Ltd
Garfield House
86–88 Edgware Road
London, W2 2EA
United Kingdom
www.newhollandpublishers.com

ISBN 10: 1-84537-686-2
ISBN 13: 978-1-84537-686-4

© This edition Roli & Janssen BV 2006
Published in India by
Roli Books in arrangement with
Roli & Janssen BV, The Netherlands
M-75, Greater Kailash-II Market
New Delhi 110 048, India.
Phone: ++91-11-29212271, 29212782
Fax: ++91-11-29217185
Email: roli@vsnl.com
Website: rolibooks.com

Editor: Priya Kapoor
Design: Sneha Pamneja
Layout: Naresh Mondal

Printed and bound in Thailand

PAGE 1: Cigarette case, gold with an enamel portrait of Maharaja Ghanshyamsinhji of Dhranghadra. Made by an unidentified European jeweller for the maharaja, c. 1930.

PREVIOUS PAGES 2-3: Pierre Arpels with Maharani Sita Devi of Baroda and her son Sayajirao Gaekwad, Paris, 1960. The jeweller shows Sita Devi a necklace set with a 34.64 carat Golconda diamond named 'Princie' in honour of her son.

FOR

BANSRI, GAURI, LEKHA,
SHAMINA AND SHEIDA

Necklace, platinum with diamonds and emeralds. Made by Van Cleef & Arpels
for Maharani Sita Devi of Baroda, 1949-50.

CONTENTS

FACING PAGE: Design for a woman's shoulder ornament with diamonds, emeralds and pearls; watercolour and gouache on paper. By Joseph Chaumet, c. 1910.

FOREWORD AND ACKNOWLEDGEMENTS

∾ᴕᴄᴖ

In a *Sunday Express* article of 1928 Maharaja Bhupinder Singh of Patiala (r. 1900-38) queried British public opinion, which held that Indian princes 'have nothing else to do except live in luxury and spend money with a shovel'.[1] Indeed, in western eyes India's princes have always appeared inconceivably rich. The very word maharaja conjures up images of fantasy. From the initial point of contact, Europeans at Indian courts were overwhelmed by the splendour of India's princes, whose absolutist attitudes and extravagance seemed without precedent at home. The spectacle of Indian kingship seldom failed to impress Europeans even if, in political terms, it was they that had the upper hand. From the late 18th century onwards the Indian subcontinent fell under British domination. With the borders of their kingdoms guaranteed under *Pax Britannica*, India's princes were no longer burdened by the expense of maintaining armies or waging war. They were now able to devote their revenues to building projects and to the acquisition of luxury goods. As feudatories in a broader British Empire, it followed that Indian princes came to emulate dominant western patterns of behaviour. The Government encouraged this westernisation process as they saw it as a means of securing the allegiance of Indian princes. The development of a new, modern, Indian princely identity was accompanied by a surge of spending on the trappings of western life. Sparing no expense, maharajas became leading patrons of luxury houses in London and Paris, commissioning the finest products of European workshops and the latest work of European artists and designers. Commissioning architects to design palaces in modern or historic-revival styles, ordering fleets of cars and resetting family jewels by the most skilled goldsmiths of the day, Indian princes established themselves as the new creative patrons of European high design. Their purchases did not stop at western-style goods alone; maharajas also commissioned from European firms articles that reflected their own traditions.

This book attempts to bring together a range of works made for Indian princes by western artists and designers. The pieces themselves are visually interesting and are highly significant as examples of princely taste. But even more important is what they reveal about the westernising process and the extent to which maharajas looked to Europe to satisfy their appetite for luxury goods. This volume is intended as a general introduction to the subject. The material included in the book has depended largely on the extent to which objects and information about them have survived. To some extent archival material on princely shopping in Europe cannot be linked to actual objects. The reverse is also true; many objects survive which were clearly made in the West for maharajas but about which little can be firmly established. Attempts have been made to secure access to records and accounts of firms which regularly supplied Indian princes. Successes in this endeavour have depended largely on the extent to which company records have been preserved. Many manufacturers and retailers with archives have helped by sharing information about their Indian commissions. But not every firm has been in a position to assist with this project; war damage, negligence or lack of interest in company history have meant that in some case there are no records to speak of. Because of this, many important suppliers to Indian princes simply cannot be represented in this volume.

This book has been made possible thanks to a large number of people. Above all, I would like to express my gratitude to Pramod Kapoor of Roli Books, who first approached me with the idea of jointly producing a book on the subject of western goods made for Indian princes. The project has been a rewarding one on many levels and I owe enormous thanks to Pramod and his team. Priya Kapoor has been a constant source of help in sourcing images and advising on the structure of the book and I owe her enormous thanks, as I do to Deepika Ahlawat and Kritika Kakkar, both of whom kindly assisted with object and archival research in London. John Fasal and Sharada Dwivedi have generously shared their knowledge with me on this subject of mutual interest. Great thanks are also due to Father Antony Alexander, Hubert Bari, Tim Best, Michael Binyon, David Bordes, Christopher Buyers, Nicholas Courtney, Anna Dallapiccola, Harry Fane, Anne Garde, Gareth Harris, Russell Harris, Niall Hobhouse, Peter Lang, Rosie Lewellyn-Jones, Colin Maitland, Anil Mulchandani, Geoffrey Munn, Dr Reto Niggl, Hansdev Patel, Dheeraj Paul, Katherine Prior, Simon Reynolds, Adrian Sassoon, Martand Singh, Rajoo Solanky, Christian Sulger-Büel, Wynyard Wilkinson, Haydn Williams and George Worlock.

In Europe and America I would like to express my thanks to: Oliver Watson at the Ashmolean Museum; Michaela Lerch and Sandrine Fritz at Baccarat; Steve Lanham at the National Motor Museum at Beaulieu; Glennys Wild at Birmingham City Museum and Art Gallery; Eric Knowles at Bonhams; M Tonnelot and Claudine Sablier at Boucheron; Howard Coutts at the Bowes Museum; Jennifer Howes at the British Library; Judy Rudoe at the British Museum; Mariola McLeod, Michel Aliaga and Veronique Sacuto at Cartier; Beatrice de Plinvil and Mélanie Sallois at Chaumet; Laura Lindsay, David Warren, Menaka Kumari Sagar, Charlotte Grant and Lynda McLeod at Christie's; Albert Bouilhet and Magali Lacroix at Christofle; Wolfgang Rabus at Daimler-Chrysler; Jane Spillman at the Corning Museum of Glass; Christopher Allen at Ede and Ravenscroft; Stefania Ricci at Ferragamo; Andrea Tanner at Fortnum & Mason; Paul Dyson at the Goldsmiths' Company; Sebastian Wormell at Harrods; Angus Cundey and Keith Levett at Henry Poole & Co.; Philip Hall at The Sir Henry Royce Memorial Foundation; Ménéhould De Bazelaire at Hermès; Daryl Greatrex at Holland & Holland; Sophie Grossiord at the Musée Galliera, Paris; Anders Ditlev Clausager at the Jaguar Daimler Heritage Trust; Zahra Kassim-Lakha at Jaeger-LeCoultre; John Hunter Lobb at John Lobb; Anne-Catherine Grimal, Elise Van Middelem and Jasmine Abdellatif at Louis Vuitton; Daria Desombre at Mauboussin; Justine Sambrook at RIBA; Jacqueline Smith at Royal Crown Derby; Susan Scott at The Savoy Hotel, London; Peter Lang and Julia Clarke at Sotheby's; Peter Lippiatt at Smythson; Pam Woolliscroft at the Spode Museum Trust; Rumi Verjee and Jim Gill at Thomas Goode; Catherine Cariou at Van Cleef & Arpels; Nick Barnard, Juliette Dugat, Clare Philips, Sonnet Stanfill, Sue Stronge, Barry Wood and Hilary Young at the Victoria and Albert Museum; Roxanne Peters and Stephanie Fawcett at V&A Images; Geoffrey Munn at Wartski; Lynn Miller at the Wedgewood Museum and Wendy Cook at the Worcester Porcelain Museum.

In India great thanks are due to the following people: in Baroda, Maharaja Ranjit Singh Gaekwad, Maharani Subhangini Rajye, Yuvarani Radhika Rajye and Manda Hingurao of the Maharaja Fatehsingh Museum Trust; in Barwani, Manvendra Singh; in Bikaner, Princess Rajyashree Kumari of Bikaner and Th. Dalip Singh and Govind Singh of the Maharaja Ganga Singh Trust; Bapa Dhrangadhara; in Jodhpur Maharaja Gaj Singh II, Yuvaraj Shivraj Singh, Baiji Lal Shivranjani Rajye, Shobha Kanwar Baiji, Dhananajaya Singh and Nikhilendra Singh; in Kapurthala, Brig. Sukhjit Singh Kapurthala; Tikka Shatrujit Singh Kapurthala; Kirat Singh of Nabha and family; and Indra Vikram Singh of Rajpipla. Many thanks are also due to Sneha Pamneja, who is responsible for the beautiful design of the book.

Office of Private Secretary.

SUBJECT.

His Highness' Visit to Europe.

"List of Purchases"

1930

GPB 219—11-29—500 PS.

8485

INTRODUCTION

୬୬ଚ⌒

'EVER SINCE I CAN REMEMBER IT WAS MY GREATEST
AMBITION TO TRAVEL IN WESTERN COUNTRIES, AND
JUDGE FOR MYSELF THE MARVELLOUS THINGS THAT
WERE TOLD ME CONCERNING THEM.'

Maharaja Jagatjit Singh of Kapurthala,
My Travels in Europe and America, 1895.

FACING PAGE: Cover page for a file on the purchases made in Europe by Maharaja Ganga Singh of Bikaner, 1930.

The great Mughal ruler Akbar (r. 1556-1605) first encountered Europeans in 1573, during his conquest of Gujarat, whose cosmopolitan ports had attracted Portuguese traders from the early 16th century. While little is known about the conversation between the ruler and the *farangis* he met, one thing is clear: the emperor emerged from the audience excited by the curious western goods that the Europeans had presented to him. Such was his fascination for the art and technology of Europe that a few years later he sent Haji Habibu-llah Kashi on a mission to Portuguese Goa expressly to bring back 'wonderful things' from the West.[1] The types of western objects that excited the imperial imagination included not only paintings, sculpture, musical instruments, weapons and exotic animals, but also examples of European clothing.[2] In subsequent years, when ambassadors from the West came to the Mughal court to negotiate alliances and trade agreements, they found that smooth relations with the emperor often relied on satisfying his strong appetite for western goods.[3] Indeed, the diplomatic treaty negotiated between James I (r. 1603-25) and the Mughal Emperor Jahangir (r. 1605-27) specified that in return for the right to trade in Hindustan the English were required to 'bring and furnish the said almighty King with all the rarietyes yearly that they can find.'[4] European articles received at court influenced the production of palace workshops, encouraging a unique fusion of western and Indian aesthetics.

The appreciation of western arts and manufactures was not confined to the imperial court. Novelties from Europe were avidly prized by rulers throughout India, who admired them for their intrinsic qualities and valued them as symbols of power and majesty.[5] Indians in positions of authority were routinely given western goods by Europeans hoping to secure preferable conditions of trade. East India Company (known as John Company, or simply the Company) documents provide an idea of what these were. In 1693 Zulfikar Khan received from Nathaniel Higginson, Governor of Madras (r. 1692-98) '2 small prospective glasses, 2 looking glasses, 1 pair Pistols…1 wax Image in glass and 2 glass globes'.[6] A few years later, Governor Thomas Pitt (1653-1726) presented 'Gopal Naick', 'a considerable man in this country', five yards of fine scarlet broadcloth, a sword blade, and two looking glasses, and gifts from the Company to the Mughal Emperor Furrukhsiyar (r. 1713-19) in 1715 included 'a table clock set with precious stones', a unicorn's horn, a gold writing cabinet and a map of the world.[7] Examples of European furniture were also offered, such as an English table and cabinet worth £70, which were presented to the Governor of Surat by the Company in 1636.[8] A letter of 1708 from a palace steward, Ziya-ud-din Khan, to the Governor and Council at Madras reveals that above all Indian rulers prized clocks and watches.[9]

The desirability of European objects was certainly felt in the adornment of some courtly interiors from as early as the second half of the 16th century. Immediately appropriated into the repertoire of luxury goods used by Indian elites were European objects with instant decorative appeal and for which local manufacture offered no alternative. Looking-glasses, for example, far superior to the polished metal mirrors hitherto used in India, were very much sought after, their size and quality permitting them to be used both for decorative and cosmetic purposes. During his stay in India in the 1750s, John-Henry Grose noted that the Indians he met 'all like European looking glasses, which are what they chiefly hang their rooms with.'[10] Markets for mirrors existed throughout India, inspiring the Company to send a Robert Young to Surat in 1614 expressly to instruct factors there in the art of silvering flat glass.[11] The Aina Mahal, a palace in Bhuj, Kutch is a rare surviving example of the Indian princely taste for mirrors and other western goods.[12] The product of a fruitful working relationship between Lakhpatji, ruler of Kutch (r. 1741-60) and a Gujarati craftsman, Ram Singh Malam, who had been largely trained in the Netherlands, the decoration of the Aina Mahal echoes European palace interiors, particularly in its central *galerie des glaces*. The ceilings are hung with chandeliers imported from Venice, and the floor is of blue and white tiles made in Bhuj after Delftware examples. Under Lakhpatji's patronage, Ram Singh and his Kutchi apprentices returned to Europe on two occasions to develop their skills and to purchase western luxury goods for their patron. These included not only chandeliers and glass, but pictures and prints, including Hogarth's *Marriage à la Mode* (1745). The Aina Mahal contains the earliest known interior by an Indian craftsman working for an Indian prince in a western style. However, it is important to keep in mind the spirit in which the palace was commissioned. Its design was not motivated by the forces of politics and westernisation which inspired palace architecture throughout India in the second half of the 19th century. Nor was it conceived by a western architect or engineer, or built to reflect a shift towards western-style living. Rather, it was the result of the Kutchi ruler's taste for western goods, an aesthetic that parallels the European taste for the exotic which existed at the same time. Just as Chinoiserie in Europe was a creation of the imagination, so was Lakhpatji's *Farangi* or 'Frankish' palace a playful Indian fantasy of the West.[13] The Aina Mahal indicates that even before it was politically expedient for them to do so, Indian princes demonstrated a keen interest in European things, which they collected and prized in precisely the same way that rare and wondrous objects from Asia were in the West.

Princely taste and the rise of
British power in India, 1750-1850

With the rise of European power in India the ownership and use of western goods assumed a different meaning. Indian princes found themselves increasingly having to accommodate and entertain Europeans on equal terms, for which they sometimes built separate western-style reception rooms. The shift in the balance of power was the result of numerous factors. The gradual disintegration of the Mughal Empire from the early years of the 18th century led to a scramble for territory in which rival powers and provincial governors, although still technically in the allegiance of the emperor, laid claim to land for themselves. Commercial and military rivalries between Britain and France assumed local significance in the subcontinent as both powers formed alliances with native rulers. In southern India, French and British forces supported rival claimants to the governorship of the Carnatic, and after a series of brilliant victories, Robert Clive (1725-74) installed the British candidate, Muhammed Ali Wallajah as nawab of Arcot (r. 1750-95; p. 32). British successes in southern India were surpassed by events in Bengal. There, Nawab Siraj-ud-daula (r. 1756-57), provoked by the East India Company's refusal to disarm, attacked Calcutta, destroying much of the city and locking up his prisoners in the jail at Fort William, a small room already then known as the Black Hole. Clive retook the city, and after defeating the nawab at the Battle of Plassey (1757), replaced him with his own candidate, Mir Jafar (r. 1757-60 & 1763-65), who agreed to relinquish military control of the province to the Company's troops. Mir Jafar expressed his gratitude to those who had enthroned him with enormous presents which consisted of cash as well as trade monopolies and exemptions from customs duties. However, senior Company servants ultimately ousted him in favour of Mir Kassim (r. 1760-63), who was in turn deposed at the Battle of Buxar (1764), at which the British defeated the combined forces of the Mughal Emperor Shah Alam II (r. 1761-1805) and Shuja-ud-daula, Nawab of Oudh (r. 1754-75; p. 34). Thereafter the Company assumed direct control of Bengal's finances, and through the Treaty of Allahabad (1765) obtained from the emperor the right to collect the revenues of Bengal, Bihar and Orissa. This influx of capital permitted the Company to support the large numbers of troops required to sustain its new position. The substantial standing army further supported the expansion of British power in the subcontinent.

This period is marked by a dramatic shift in the Company's activities in India. Originally established for the purpose of trade, by the late 18th century the East India Company began to assume the characteristics of a political power, a role formalised by Lord Wellesley (1760-1842), Governor-General from 1797 to 1805. Together, the defeat and death of the pro-French Tipu Sultan of Mysore (r. 1782-99), the conquest of Delhi in 1803 and the end of the Third Maratha War in 1818 delivered control of the subcontinent into British hands. Sikh power too was decisively checked by 1849, and the Company also annexed without provocation the states of Sindh in 1843 and Oudh in 1856. Defeated states were effectively carved up to suit Company interests while loyal princes and those who simply accepted British hegemony were bound by subsidiary treaties in which they surrendered control over their foreign policy and renounced their right to maintain armies. The agreements guaranteed 'perpetual friendship, alliance and a unity of interests' between the Company and individual princes, who acknowledged British supremacy and ceased to operate as sovereign powers.[14]

Indian princes allied to the various western trading companies showed a taste for western goods that reflected their political loyalties. On a practical level too, Indian elites who negotiated and fraternised with Europeans eventually began to adopt aspects of western lifestyle and behaviour, such as sitting on a chair instead of on textiles on the ground. An example is found in Muhammed Ali Wallajah, Nawab of Arcot, whose very position depended on the support of East India

Company officials. The nawab was entangled in complex financial dealings with the British community, whom he liberally entertained in Madras at Chepauk Palace, whose western-style reception rooms, were filled with English furniture, pier glasses and paintings. These had been ordered in 1767 from London through the agencies of Nicholas Morse, Governor of Madras from 1744-46.[15] The nawab's European friends were regularly called on to execute his demands for western goods, which ranged from the latest mechanical devices and automata to eyeglasses.[16] The ruler also commissioned works from western artists, among them splendid portraits of himself (p. 32) and his sons. Muhammed Ali also assumed aspects of western behaviour. On one occasion George Paterson (1734-1817), found him 'at the corner of his Gardens at breakfast with his family quite in the English manner. Tea, Cakes and several sorts of Salading on Table, a Cloth laid and all on Chairs.'[17] The nawab of Arcot was not isolated in his penchant for western goods. His contemporary, the ruler of Trichinopoly, hung a gallery of his palace with 'small Pictures of several of the French royal family or Nobility, and furniture all brought from Pondicherry'.[18] In the same period, Tuloji Raje, Raja of Tanjore (r. 1763-73 & 1776-87) decorated his palace with English pictures and prints, among them several portraits of George III (r. 1760-1820) and Queen Charlotte (1744-1818).[19]

Even before the establishment of the Raj in 1858, Indian palace interiors were regularly embellished with decorative articles from Europe, as was observed by writers of the period. Mary Martha Sherwood (1775-1851), for example, found that the palace of Mubarak-ud-Daula, Nawab of Bengal (r. 1810-21), was 'lighted by English glass chandeliers', a dramatic departure from the candlesticks and oil lamps that would traditionally have been used.[20] Emily Eden (1797-1869) visited a palace near Agra likewise 'fitted up in the oddest way with French chandeliers of green and purple and yellow glace, as thick as they could be hung. Looking-glasses, and old-fashioned mirrors, and English prints on the walls.'[21] Fanny Parks (1794-1875) found that the palace of Lucknowi nobleman Hakim Mehndi was crammed with exotic articles from the West: 'Tables were spread all down the centre of the room, covered with most heterogeneous articles: round the room were glass cases, full of clocks, watches, sundials, compasses, guns, pistols, swords; every thing you can imagine might be found in these cases.'[22]

The impact of the West also extended to lifestyle. Living at Vizagapatam in the 1820s, Sir Jasper Nicholls (1778-1849) was delighted to learn that Narayana Babu, Raja of Vizianagram (r. 1794-1845), not only spoke and wrote English, but was also learning how to play the piano.[23] As with many Indian rulers in spheres of western influence, the raja regularly invited European guests to participate in palace celebrations. Such events were invariably awkward as both parties grappled with the etiquette and customs of the other. Mrs Sherwood found that at dinner with the nawab of Bengal the guests 'used their knives and forks as if they had never handled either before'.[24] For dinners given by Raja Govind Baksh, plates and cutlery were furnished by one of the guests since these are 'not known in the east, where they always eat, and even help you, with the right hand'.[25] A shortage of cutlery and plate was certainly not a problem at the court of Lucknow, whose rulers were embroiled in complex political dealings with the Company and consequently entertained British officials on a regular basis. The nawabs of Oudh had an extensive collection of western goods. These were sometimes obtained from Europeans at court, who undertook shopping trips to Calcutta on their behalf, as did J. Munro Sinclair, who was sent off to buy carriages, silver spectacles and china baths in 1827.[26] In 1796 Claude Martin (1735-1800) ordered through his London agents William and Thomas Raikes a host of goods for Nawab Asaf-ud-daula (r. 1775-97).[27] These included gold-plated pocket knives in cases, scissors, razors, nail-cutters, betel-nut cutters, spectacles, magnifying glasses, surgical and dissecting instruments as well as 'trinkets' from Mathew Boulton's manufactory in Birmingham. The purchase of European goods by Indian rulers enriched the merchants and tradesmen through whom they were ordered, who typically received a commission on such transactions. So extravagant were the nawabs of Oudh that Lucknow became a magnet for anyone in possession of European novelties. An example is found in clockmaker Victor Malliardet, who obtained leave from the East India Company to travel to Lucknow in 1796 in order to sell Nawab Asaf-ud-daula £4,000 worth of automata, among them a 'young lady playing the harpsichord, also a small snuffbox from which a little bird would spring up, give several natural tones and shut himself up again in the box'.[28]

European visitors to Lucknow were astonished by the style in which the nawabs entertained their foreign guests. Nawab Sadaat Ali Khan (r. 1798-1814) served them European delicacies prepared by a

French chef in a room 'furnished with chairs, and every other article in the European style'.[29] Lord Valentia's (1770-1844) description of a dinner in Lucknow during the reign of the same nawab provides an idea of the anglicised tastes of the court: 'The scene was so singular, and so contrary to all my ideas of Asiatic manners, that I could hardly persuade myself that the whole was not a masquerade. An English apartment, a band in English regimentals, playing English tunes; a room lighted by magnificent English girandoles, English tables, chairs, and looking-glasses; an English service of plates; English knives, forks, spoons, wine glasses, decanters and cut-glass vases–how could these convey any idea that we were seated in the court of an Asiatic prince?'[30] The Lucknowi penchant for western goods extended to employing skilled western artists, such as Robert Home (1752-1834), a pupil of Angelica Kaufman, who was appointed court painter to Nawab Ghazi-ud-din Haidar (r. 1814-27). When in 1818 the East India Company awarded the ruler the title of king, he engaged Home to design for him regalia and courtly paraphernalia worthy of an Anglophile Indian monarch. Home laced Oudh's heraldic twin fish into the vocabulary of Greek and Egyptian revival motifs in fantastic and sometimes implausible creations. His album of drawings, now in the Victoria and Albert Museum, London, includes sketches of extraordinary objects, including yachts, carriages and *howdahs* of ingenious and charming design.[31] Portraits of Ghazi-ud-din Haidar show him wearing a European-style crown and an ermine cloak in the manner of a European ruler (p. 33). A younger son of the Mughal Emperor Akbar II (r. 1806-37) likewise appreciated the symbolic effect of western symbols of authority and, much to the astonishment of European observers, wore a star insignia on both breasts of his European-style coat.[32]

Western-style living during the British Raj

The political and economic subjugation of the subcontinent to British interests created a deep resentment that found expression in anti-British uprisings which inflamed northern and central India in 1857-58. The suppression of this movement brought with it the end of the Mughal Empire and the exile to Burma of its last ruler, Bahadur Shah Zafar II (r. 1837-58), who had assumed the role of figurehead during the attempt to squash Company rule. The East India Company ceased to

operate, and the British Crown assumed control of India, which it exercised either through a viceroy, or through the machinery of the subcontinent's more than five hundred princely states. Years of centralised Mughal authority had created a deeply entrenched system of vassalage among the ruling powers of Hindustan. The British effectively maintained this order by adopting to some extent Mughal forms of tribute and homage. As a representative of the Crown, the viceroy therefore held durbars, granted landholdings, affirmed or awarded titles and observed court rituals such as distributing *paan* and sprinkling rosewater. The absorption of indigenous iconography and ceremony by the British reflected a broader governmental policy of inspiring loyalty among Indian princes and inviting them within the fold of the British

Empire. In 'A Proclamation to the Princes, Chiefs, and the People of India', delivered in November 1858, Queen Victoria (r. 1837-1901) pledged to 'respect the rights, dignity, and honour of native princes as our own', a guarantee that the Company policy of annexing princely states had come to an end.[33] Native rulers were thereafter treated as feudatories, carefully ranked and ordered according to importance. Princely states such as Bhopal, Patiala, Rampur, Gwalior and Hyderabad, which had remained pro-British during the uprisings of 1857 were of course rewarded with promotions and land grants.[34] All princely states of importance, termed 'First Division States', were flattered with conspicuous ceremonial symbols, among them gun salutes. The number of guns fired–which typically ranged from 9 to 21– clearly reflected a prince's status and his relative position within the imperial system; the queen herself was entitled to 101. As part of the British Empire, India's princes ceased to actively rule. No longer able to compete through conventional means of warfare and diplomacy, they increasingly employed honorific symbols as a way of articulating their power. Status symbols related directly to the degree of political power that each prince enjoyed in his state.[35] Leading princes were permitted almost total legislative and administrative independence while lesser states were given only limited autonomy.

Under the British Raj Queen Victoria replaced the Mughal emperor as the source of legitimate authority in the subcontinent. For most Indians this point was driven home on the coins they used, on which the image of the queen substituted that of the emperor.[36] Links between the Indian people and the queen were further reinforced, when, by the Royal Titles Act of 1876, she assumed the title of Empress of India. By adopting this position the queen bound herself closer to her Indian subjects, a relationship she took to heart, even to the point of learning Hindustani. For India's princes, her involvement added a personal dimension to the Raj, encouraging loyalty and fostering commitment to a royal figurehead. To commemorate the Act, Lord Lytton (1831-91) staged the first of a series of impressive durbars in Delhi in 1877, to which ninety leading princes were invited. The durbar formally incorporated the rulers into a larger British socio-political hierarchy. In visual and ceremonial terms, this was partly achieved through the awarding of armorial bearings. These had been designed by a Calcutta civil servant, Robert Taylor, drawing on information provided by the states themselves. Taylor's designs employed Indian symbols and imagery, but were configured according to the conventions of western heraldry. Prior to the bestowing of formal western-style coats of arms Indian princes had represented themselves with symbols, such as the sun (favoured by Rajputs of the *Suryavanshi* race) or the twin fish (used by the nawabs of Oudh). Before the granting of coat of arms, these symbols were sometimes used in the manner of western heraldry. Raja Rajaram of Kolhapur (r. 1866-70) even had a pair of *morchals* (peacock-feather fans), a traditional symbol of Indian royalty, engraved on his writing paper.[37] As was the case in Europe, in India coats of arms became central to the representation of princes. Emblazoned on the sides of carriages, or mounted as pennants on cars, they announced the elevated status of the bearer (pp.212-13). As a signal of rank, coats of arms were rapidly applied to the paraphernalia of courtly life. In formal Indian royal portraiture, coats of arms feature regularly, firmly declaring a prince's allegiance within a broader western-dominated political system.

A further system of honours was established for Indian princes in the form of membership to chivalric orders. Such orders were rooted in the Medieval culture of the West and were imbued with the spirit of chivalry and military brotherhood. Belonging to an order rested on a commitment to a cause and allegiance to an overlord. The birth of orders was closely linked to the protracted conflict between Christian and Islamic kingdoms, specifically in the quest of the former to liberate the Holy Land from Muslim domination. By the 19th century of course, military orders had become symbolic, with membership awarded as a favour or recognition of service and loyalty to the Crown. Dispensing orders also provided a conspicuous way of rewarding a subject without the commitment of bestowing a hereditary title or estate. As India was incorporated into the British Empire new orders were invented to help bring Indians into the British political system and to secure their loyalty. The Order of the Star of India was founded in 1861 in time to reward Indian princes who had stood loyal during the uprisings of 1857-58. In consideration for the religious of its members, the insignia was designed not in the shape of the usual cross but as a star, and the collar was devised with alternating Indian lotuses and Tudor roses interspersed with palm leaves.[38] Membership was reserved for senior Indian princes and for the most high-ranking British officials, the purpose being to unite the ruling classes of the different races into a common group. Queen Victoria herself was appointed Sovereign of the Order, and the viceroy assumed the post of Grand Master. The Star of India was complimented in 1877 by the less exclusive Order of the Indian Empire, which carried the motto '*Imperatricis auspiciis*' ('Under the auspices of the Empress') and was intended to recognise the work of important Indian and senior British officials for long-standing exemplary service. To acknowledge the role of women of the Raj, in 1878 another order was created, that of the Imperial Order of the Crown of India, which included the Sovereign herself as well as wives of princes, notable Indian ladies and wives of the most high-ranking British officials in India. State portraits of princes under the Raj frequently showed them wearing the mantle and insignia of these honours, thereby emphasising their loyalty to the Crown.

In addition to orders, the Crown liberally elevated rajas (kings) to the rank of maharaja (great king), eventually somewhat devaluing the significance of this lofty title.[39] While the British Government happily heaped titles and honours on Indian princes, they equally made it clear that maharajas were not on equal footing with European royalty. In official correspondence and documentation from the late 19th century onwards, Indian princes were increasingly described as 'native chiefs', effectively depriving them of royal rank. Under Lord Curzon (1859-1925), viceroy from 1898-1905, special pains were taken to ensure that Indian rulers did not 'ape the insignia of royalty'.[40] A particularly sore point was the arched crown. With the rise of British power, some princes had taken to wearing metal or textile western-style crowns instead of traditional turbans. In protecting the sacred identity of the Royal Family, the Government barred Indian princes from donning anything resembling a European crown. An example may be found in official records dated 1912 which condemned the behaviour of Bhupinder Singh, Maharaja of Patiala (r. 1900-38):[41]

> On the 24th January there was a Durbar in Patiala at which he wore a diamond crown made in England, just like the crown of European kings. He wore it without a pugree or turban just like a king. This is new departure in Patiala. The crown is worth 20 lakhs and most of the old gems are set up in it. All the Sikhs both of old and new schools do not like the Maharaja's appearing without a turban and are displeased.

Princes overcame the anti-crown ruling in different ways. Members of some royal houses for example, simply wore tiaras over their turbans, thus simulating the glitter and regal effect of a crown without technically crossing governmental policy.[42] Officials were also instructed to reprimand those rulers who used on their letterhead and insignia arched crowns that might be confused with the 'Royal Crown of England'. The rulers of Cooch Behar, Dhar, Kapurthala, Nabha and Rampur were duly chastised, although ultimately it proved impossible to suppress the use of this potent royal symbol, in print at least.[43] The Government also attempted to prevent maharajas from awarding medals and establishing their own military honours, a point that was much contested by Indian princes. Although a compromise was reached on this matter, and maharajas were allowed to distribute medals, these could only be given to their own subjects and could not 'clash or compare' with medals or orders conferred by the Crown.[44] In all instances the Government operated on the basis that 'nothing should be done which might create the impression that there can be any fountain of Imperial honour other than the King-Emperor and his representative.'[45]

Within each princely state British interests were articulated through a resident or political agent, a Crown representative who monitored the ruler's behaviour and ensured that Government directives were duly followed. Although on the whole, treaty terms specified that the Crown would not interfere in domestic affairs, in reality both matters of state and the personal conduct of rulers were often regulated by London.[46] The Crown endorsed or prevented marriages, recognised or disapproved of heirs, approved or barred rights to travel, and ultimately bestowed and withdrew the right to sit on the throne. Due to the restrictions imposed on them, princes found that relations with the British were seldom easy. Irrespective of his behaviour, to his subjects a prince was a sacred figure who ruled by divine right. By contrast, the official British view was that an Indian ruler had to uphold certain moral and political standards in order to retain his position. In accordance with the belief that 'the quality of rule depends first and foremost on the character of the Prince', Crown policy was to remove young rulers and heirs-apparent from the influence of the zenana and to have them educated in a western style.[47] An example of the heavy-handed approach taken by Government in questions of education is found in the young Raja Rajagopala of Pudukkottai (r. 1928-72). When, in 1930, the ruler's mother insisted that her son be educated by Hindu religious teachers she was declared unfit to govern the child and her allowance was cut.[48] Likewise, when Rajaram of Kolhapur came to throne at the age of sixteen, the Government immediately removed him from his family and installed him in a house near the Residency, where he was taught western habits, such as playing billiards and reading English newspapers.[49]

Government-approved English tutors became a standard feature in palace households, where they were meant to follow a western-style public-school curriculum and to instruct princes in western manners. Tutors were sometimes influential figures, becoming advisors and companions to their pupils. Royal children also received instruction from Indian teachers. In her memoirs, Gayatri Devi, Rajmata of Jaipur (b. 1919) reveals something about her childhood lessons in Cooch Behar: '…we had an English governess, Miss Hobart, to teach us English, English history and literature, and some French, and two Bengali tutors, one for mathematics and Indian history and the other for Bengali and Sanskrit.'[50] Invariably challenges arose as British tutors had to teach their royal students to think along western lines, without fundamentally

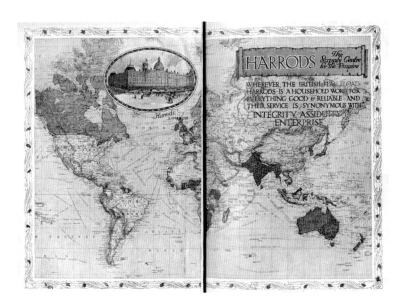

18

challenging their traditional values. As his tutor, Austin Robinson (1897-1993) remembered the young Maharaja George Jiyajirao Scindia of Gwalior (r. 1925-61) telling him plainly: 'Sahib, it is not my job to make you a Hindu; it is not your job to make me a Christian. It is my job to make you a good Christian.'[51] In order to ensure that princes received a similar upbringing and to promote collegiate values, schools were established throughout India for the sons of rulers. Mayo College in Ajmer (1875), Rajkumar College in Rajkot (1868), Rajkumar College in Jabalpur (1882: moved to Raipur in 1894), Aitchison College in Lahore (1886) and Daly College in Indore (1882) all turned out princes and nobles who were gentlemen, spoke perfect English, played cricket and socialised on easy terms with Europeans. These attributes were especially true for princes who were sent to England to complete their studies at schools such as Eton or Harrow, Oxford or Cambridge, and who returned home completely westernised.

Within one generation of western education the lifestyle of India's princes were transformed and they began to wear western clothes, engage in western games and eat western food.[52] In her memoirs, Brinda Devi of Kapurthala (1890-1962) vividly recalls the first time she wore a western-style dress, and learned 'to eat my meals at a table like Europeans instead of Indian-fashion on the floor'.[53] The repercussions of such a shift in behaviour were evident on many levels. First and foremost, those princes who could afford it abandoned their traditional residences for new, substantial palaces principally designed by western architects. These were built in a variety of styles, from Baronial to Palladian revival and Indo-Saracenic. Although they included spaces for traditional courtly activities such as durbar, the critical point about these palaces is that they were built to accommodate western-style living, with its specific rooms for dining, sleeping, socialising, sport and recreation. The western-style elevated furniture and domestic articles needed to outfit these new vast palaces were readily supplied by British firms such as Maples & Co. and Waring & Gillow, both of which had showrooms in India. Businesses such as these saw British consumers in India as their principal market but were equally able to cater to princely clients, for whom they supplied furnishings that were both imported and locally-made under European supervision. From the early 19th century British household goods and necessaries were increasingly available in India and these included everything from nuts and bolts and cricket bats, cuckoo clocks, pickles and cheeses.[54] The development of mail-order, a system of purchasing goods by correspondence, ensured that even consumers in the remotest corners of the Empire could rely on safe delivery of everything they needed in daily life. Businesses with an eye on the Indian market also produced articles specifically designed to appeal to local tastes, both in form and style. For western firms making luxury goods, be it F&C Osler, Baccarat, Cartier, Boucheron, Louis Vuitton, Holland & Holland or Rolls-Royce, Indian princes proved to be substantial clients and at certain times, such as during the Great Depression, were the mainstay of business.

Increasing westernisation substantially changed relationships between princes and the Europeans they encountered. The diary of English portraitist Emily Merrick (b. 1842) provides an insight into the easy exchange that she enjoyed with the westernised princes whom she met. Among these were Nripendra Narayan of Cooch Behar (r. 1863-1911), who had been partly educated in England, and whose wife Sunity Devi (1864-1932), was the daughter of the Brahmo Samaj leader Keshab Chandra Sen. Merrick regularly met the Cooch Behars in Calcutta for 'tennis and dinner parties'.[55] The maharaja, who was 'very English in all his tastes and pursuits' impressed his guests with his talents on the playing field and in the ballroom, where he 'is always seen to be dancing with the prettiest English ladies'. Ananda Gajapathi Raju, ruler of Vizianagram (r. 1879-97), was no less impressive, being a 'cultivated and well-read man, speaking French as well as English, and in his conversation often quoting Shakespeare.'[56] The western education given to Sayajirao III of Baroda had positive consequences for his state. The progressive ruler instituted laws to help overcome social discrimination, he promoted compulsory primary schooling, fought for the emancipation of women and established laws to prevent child marriage. His wife, Chimnabai II (1872-1958) co-authored *The Position of Women in Indian Life* (1911), and the couple educated their sons and daughter in Europe.

Western education also created complications. Princes were somehow expected to think along western lines without themselves becoming so westernised that they lost touch with their own traditions and people. An example of attendant obstacles may be found in the case of Raja Martanda Tondiman of Pudukkottai (r. 1886-1928). An official report of 1897 noted that 'The Raja is more a coloured European gentleman, with entirely European tastes, than a Native Prince.'[57] Following his marriage to Melbourne-born Molly Fink and the birth of a son, he was encouraged to abdicate and ultimately settled in Cannes.[58] Muhammed Iftikhar Ali Khan, Nawab of Pataudi (r. 1917-52) himself found that the 'English upbringing' he was given made it difficult for him to relate to and understand his Indian subjects.[59] The sons of Nripendra Narayan of Cooch Behar and his wife Sunity Devi were educated in England and returned home fluent in English and French, but unable to speak Sanskrit, Urdu or Bengali.[60] Girls raised in a western style found it no easier to conform to traditional Indian life. Indira Devi of Cooch Behar (1892-1968), for instance, was educated in a western manner, and having been taught to think for herself, found it impossible to accept Indian conventions such as arranged marriage.[61] For westernised princesses, it was particularly problematic straddling their modern education with the oppressive convention of purdah. In some states a clean break was made with purdah, such as at Baroda, where Sayajirao III abolished the practice in 1913. In some instances, royal ladies lived out of purdah while abroad, but in purdah while at home. Begum Kaikhusrau Jahan of Bhopal (r. 1901-26), however, observed strict purdah even when abroad. Rosita Forbes recalls how on state occasions in Europe she 'surmounted the *Burkha* enjoined by Moslem tradition with the most magnificent diamond crown and a profusion of necklaces of the same precious stones.'[62] On her trip to Europe in 1925, Maharani Badan Kanwarji Sahiba of Jodhpur (1905-75) likewise kept purdah, travelling around London in a curtained Rolls-Royce and doing her shopping at Harrods in the evening, where by special arrangement she was served exclusively by salesgirls.

Indian Princes in Europe

The Government encouraged those princes who were sufficiently rich to travel to Britain. Initially these visits had a didactic purpose, the idea being that a tour of the mother country would inspire rulers to replicate high British standards in governance and social policy. Leading princes were also sometimes invited to London to participate in coronations and jubilee celebrations, at which they represented India. Not every prince was deemed worthy of such an honour. When twenty-two year old Martanda of Pudukkottai applied for permission to attend Queen Victoria's Diamond Jubilee celebrations in 1897, he was flatly refused. The Government felt strongly that the visit, 'in company with many richer Chiefs' would incur expenses that he could not sustain. Besides this, the young ruler was already 'inclined to extravagance…which a visit to England cannot but tend to accentuate.'[63] The raja responded furiously, 'Is this the treatment I deserve after all my forefathers' services to British Government?' He pressed his claim by arguing that 'A visit to England would be fitting completion to my Education which has been on English lines.' Even if the Government agreed, there was no guarantee that a ruler's own family would permit him to break Hindu

19

strictures and cross the *kaala-pani* (literally 'black water'). To some, fears about traversing the ocean seemed justified when, in 1870, a prince who ignored the advice of his priests and travelled to Europe, Rajaram of Kolhapur, died in Florence on his way home to India (p. 19). Twenty-five years later, when Bijay Chand Mahtab, ruler of Burdwan (r. 1881-1941), announced his plans to visit Europe he was told to cancel his plans by a senior prince who warned him that such a trip was an 'Un-Hindu thing to do'.[64]

Planning a trip required considerable effort, in particular selecting the vast staff that invariably travelled in a ruler's entourage.

Practical travel arrangements were most often undertaken by the agents T. Cook & Sons. Princes also needed the services of a European companion who could provide correct advice on finer points of etiquette. For instance, when Shahu Bhonsle, ruler of Kolhapur (1874-1922) went to Europe to attend the coronation of Edward VII (r. 1901-10), he was assisted by Sir Claude Hill, in whose honour he later built a sanitarium.[65] Kolhapur began preparing himself for the journey by dining at home 'for a few days in English fashion' but his plans were thwarted by a community of Brahmin priests, who used this lapse of behaviour to discredit the ruler. In the end he expressed a concern that in spite of his desire to learn western ways 'the change, I am afraid, would be so sudden and so great that we may find it difficult to leave at once the habits which are born with us.'[66] One Indian traveller found that the lengthy shipboard journey to Europe offered sufficient time to

assimilate western habits, and provided an environment where 'nobody minds your little short-comings'.[67] A pleasant surprise that awaited Indians going abroad was the relative absence of racism. One Indian traveller going to Europe in the early 20th century was delighted to find on the steamer that the waiters 'did not make any distinction between a native and a European'.[68]

Food was a particular concern for Indians travelling abroad, not only because of differences in cuisine, but because in Hinduism the purity of food could only be maintained if it was prepared according to strict rules. According to Hindu principles, food could be handled only

INDIAN AND ANGLO-INDIAN DISHES

FOR OUR JUBILEE VISITORS

Prepared in strict accordance with Hindu caste and Mohammedan requirements. Dishes or complete meals supplied daily at your residence or hotel. Turbaned waiters £1 1 0.

A FEW SPECIMEN DISHES

SHOORVAS, RUSSAMS (Soups)
Consommé Mulligatawny, Mulligatawny (Madras Pepper Water), Khavard (Fish), Tharkari (Vegetable) Mulligatawny, Dhal Shoorva   from 6/- a dish

PILLAUS AND BIRIANNIES
Lamb Pillau, Mutton Pillau, Koftah Pillau, Ginga, (Prawn) Pillau, Tharkari (Vegetable) Pillau   from 22/-

CURRIES AND DOPIAZAS
(Madras, Bengal, Malay and Ceylon)
All kinds of Meat Curries, English or Indian Vegetables, Lady's Fingers, Fish, Egg, Plain or with Dhal   from 16/-

KHABAB CURRY
(either plain or on Sticks)
Koftah Curry (Ball Curry), Kheema or Minced Meat Curries (Plain or with Vegetables)   16/-

DRY CURRIES
Country Captain of Chicken, Chundole, Madras   from 16/-

KABABS   from 16/-

KORMAS   from 16/-

MOLEYS   from 20/-

BURTHAS AND SAMBALS   6/-

SPECIAL ANGLO-INDIAN DISHES
Brinjal Cutlets, Chicken Cutlets, Potato Chops, Brain Cutlets, Sweetbread Cutlets, Indian Savoury Stews, Foogath   12/-

ROTIES   1/- each

BHUGIAS
(Savory Pastries)   8/-

POOREES AND GOOLGOOLAS   6d. each

MEETAI
Hulwa (different kinds and flavours), Dhood Padah, Burfi (different kinds and flavours), Khoa or Kovah, Jellabis, Goolab Jamon, Copra Meetai   7/- a lb.

DHAI, 2/- a jar; GHEE, 4/- a jar; MALAI, packed in ½ lb. screw topped jars, 2/- a jar; AND RICE from 2/8 a packet

All dishes sufficient for 4 persons

13

20

by people of equal or higher caste; contact with Europeans polluted food and its recipient. Rajaram of Kolhapur therefore travelled around Europe with his own cooks who carried rice, spices and vessels from home.[69] Gaekwar Sayajirao III of Baroda travelled to Europe with his own cooks, groceries and two cows, while his contemporary Maharaja Madho Singh of Jaipur (r. 1880-1922) set off for Edward VII's coronation in 1901 with four silver urns, each filled with 9,000 litres of *Ganga jal*, sacred drinking water from the River Ganges.[70] Those who attempted western food, or worse, curries served in European restaurants, were seldom pleased. Nawab Mehdi Hasan of Hyderabad was shocked by the 'detestably bad' food he ate during his stay in Paris, and was outraged by the prices charged for it.[71] One Indian traveller concluded simply that although French cuisine was superior to English, the cooks of both 'ought not to hesitate to take lessons from the Indian.'[72] Those who travelled to England without a cook developed cravings for their own cuisine. In London it was always possible to dine at the East India United Services Club, which served curry to its members, principally retired Raj officials.[73] One early 20th century Indian visitor to London found that a Mr Fateh Mohamed had opened an Indian restaurant with turbaned waiters that turned out perfectly acceptable food. He noted prophetically that 'Indian dishes such as curry and rice are coming into favour with Englishmen.'[74] By the 1930s Fortnum & Mason was supplying a range of Indian food prepared in strict accordance with caste regulations. A longing for home also took princes to places with Indian associations. Indians in London delighted in visiting the Indian section of the South Kensington Museum (renamed the Victoria and Albert Museum in 1899), which they likened to the museums at Bombay and Lahore 'but on grander scale'.[75] And visitors also found to their satisfaction that among the worthies at Madame Tussaud's were the Gaekwar of Baroda and the Begum of Bhopal.[76]

On the whole Indian princes were impressed by the grandeur of European hotels, which knew no equal in India. A Telugu traveller found that 'the palaces of our Indian princes cannot equal these hotels', an observation echoed by Mayo School graduate Bhawani Singh, ruler of Jhalawar (r. 1899-1929), who wrote from the Grand Hotel du Louvre that the life of Indian princes was poor 'compared with that of a passenger who has taken up his abode for a day or two in such a palace as this.'[77] After a stay in the English countryside Nawab Mehdi Hasan of Hyderabad remarked too that 'there is no comparison between the palaces of our princes and the houses of the English aristocracy.'[78] Such views echo a broader attitude of the superiority of Europe that Indian travellers observed in everything from the beauty of European architecture to the quality of European craftsmanship. Meherban Narayanrao Babasaheb, Chief of Ichalkaranji (1870-1943), a *jagir* in the state of Kolhapur, summarised the view of most Indian visitors to the West: 'Everything in Europe, especially England, seems to be on a larger scale than in India.'[79] London in particular, the 'biggest and richest city in the world', was seen as 'the pivot of the universe', a city worthy of the vast empire of which it was the centre.[80]

Princes travelling to the West followed a programme that almost always included visiting a few European capitals, a stay in the English countryside and a visit to Scotland. Their time in London was typically marked by sightseeing and official visits to civic institutions, the latter arranged by the India Office, the 'building under which our destinies are really decided.'[81] Some princes took the opportunity of being in the capital to improve their talents, an example being Rajaram of Kolhapur, who sought out a dancing-master to give him lessons in quadrilles.[82] Princely observations of Europe reveal much about the differences between contemporary life in India and the West. The absence of caste barriers and racism were frequently noted and appreciated.[83] Free social interactions with women was also recognised as one of the pleasures of life in Europe. European women were admired for their company and it was recognised that their presence among men enriched life, enhancing

the pleasure he gained at being the first reigning Sikh prince to express 'the devotion of our nation to Her Majesty's person and throne'.[93] The experience of meeting the queen was a profound experience for some. Sunity Devi of Cooch Behar was overcome by her meeting with this 'legendary figure endowed with wonderful attributes' who was bound to her Indian subjects by 'silken chains of love and loyalty'.[94] Nawab Mehdi Hasan felt as if in a dream, overcome by disbelief at the sight of 'that lady under whose rule I was born' and 'whom I was taught to love'.[95] His 'heart was filled with the enthusiasm of love and loyalty. Whoever would have thought that I should come across the sea many thousand miles and have the good fortune to see my beloved sovereign?' The queen's interest in her Indian subjects was also gratifying for the princes who came to see her: 'We take precedence here, both at court and in private houses. What a recompense for the humiliations we undergo in India.'[96] In some cases princes formed friendships with the British royal family. When Sunity Devi visited England for Queen Victoria's Golden Jubilee celebrations in 1887, she was warmly received at court, winning the affection of the queen herself and the friendship of her children and grandchildren. These ties were formalised, when, in 1888 the queen agreed to be godmother to Sunity's son, named Victor. George V (r. 1910-36) and Queen Mary (1867-1953) became godparents to Jivarjirao (George) and Kamalaraje (Mary), children of Maharaja Madho Rao Scindia of Gwalior (r. 1886-1925). Such links continued generation to generation and were reinforced by the state visits to Indian undertaken by members of the royal family officially representing the sovereign.

The Pleasures of Shopping

Whether buying mirrors in Venice, porcelain in Dresden or jewellery in Paris, shopping was an indispensable part of a European tour. For first-time visitors, it was essential on arrival to acquire western-style clothes. The colourful apparel of Indian princes aroused attention, and the sooner they adopted full western dress, the sooner they were able to appear inconspicuous during their travels. So outlandish was his dress considered, that while sitting on a bench in the Musée Grevin in Paris, a courtier travelling with Jagatjit Singh of Kapurthala was mistaken for one of the museum's waxwork figures![97] Indian women too sometimes

conversation and manners.[84] The beauty of European women was frequently noted, one Indian writer writing comically that while 'in India, we meet with both extremes–supremely beautiful women as well as positively ugly ones', in 'London the percentage of very ugly women is certainly small'.[85] Writers also noted similarities between Europe and India. The sight of Brighton at noon reminded Nawab Mehdi Hasan of Benares while Bijay Chand Mahtab, ruler of Burdwan, found that the River Cam was much like the moat around his summer palace.[86] Problems of life in the West were also observed, among them drunkenness and materialism, traffic and the high cost of living.[87] One Indian traveller noted that baldness was more apparent in England than India and concluded simply that 'the climate and water are not favourable to the growth of hair here'![88]

As subject peoples in an imperial system there was no greater honour for an Indian prince than to meet his ruler. For formal events, such as presentation at court, Indians were instructed to wear 'proper Durbar dress' complete with national or tribal headgear.[89] It was in romantic Oriental garb that Queen Victoria and her successors wished to view the exotic peoples of the Empire.[90] As surviving negatives from London's fashionable photographic studio Lafayette show, Indians routinely called in on the way to court in order to be photographed on the day they met the sovereign.[91] For Raja Martanda his audience with Queen Victoria was 'a red letter day in the annals of Pudukkottai'.[92] Maharaja Jagatjit Singh of Kapurthala (r. 1877-1949) related in his diary adopted western clothes when travelling in Europe, as did Rani Kanari (d. 1910), wife of Jagatjit Singh of Kapurthala, and Chimnabai II, wife of Sayajirao III of Baroda.[98] The social round in London also necessitated particular types of dress, such as an evening suit and top hat, both of which could be acquired by outfitters in and around Savile Row. For westernised princes, visits to Europe provided an opportunity to order clothes and update their wardrobes with the latest fashions. Western clothes, shoes and handbags, were also becoming an indispensable part of a royal bride's trousseau and visits to Europe provided an ideal opportunity to choose the latest creations from leading fashion houses.[99] Sayajirao III was so regular a client of Henry Poole & Co., that he awarded the company a royal warrant (p. 105). Before one of his many trips to Europe, Maharaja Ganga Singh (r. 1887-1943), the celebrated ruler of Bikaner compiled a list of the clothes he needed, among which were 'Blue tennis blazer coats, flannel tennis trousers, flannel Tennis shirts', and sweaters and ties in Bikaner state colours.[100]

The Royal Archives in Bikaner are rich with detail about the princely family's purchases during their European travels. Shopping trips were coordinated well in advance, so that the most could be achieved in the limited time. All manner of goods were required for the various royal residences, for which purpose Maharaja Ganga Singh asked his staff to prepare in advance a complete list of tradesmen in London, Paris and Marseilles, among them: silversmiths and goldsmiths, picture dealers, furniture dealers, tailors, hatters and hosiers, as well as sellers of fancy goods, leather goods, enamelled goods, bronzes, walking sticks and umbrellas, china, glass, crystal and glassware, clocks, clothes, electric fittings, garden implements, rifles, guns and cartridges and fireplace accessories.[101] Items on the shopping agenda for a 1930 visit to Europe also included stationery and leather accessories, the purchase of menu-stands and other banquet-related material, a 'weighing machine for her highness', tie and trouser presses and presents for the royal family and place staff. Maharaja Ganga Singh's private secretary also pre-ordered goods from London tradesmen, which the ruler would inspect on his arrival at the Carlton Hotel in London. In many instances the maharaja returned to his favourite shops, whose names were all carefully noted in the lists compiled during former trips, which were filed for reference. In London many of the transactions were undertaken by Messrs Biddulph Rawlins, who had the responsibility of liaising with tradesmen and settling accounts. In Paris the same function was filled by

M. Henri Irigoin. For the European visit of Ganga Singh's successor, Maharaja Sadul Singh (r. 1943-50) in 1949, long 'to-do' lists were prepared for these European agents. Messrs Biddulph Rawlins were to find soap samples in at least seven different colours, repair binoculars, source bed and table linen, sanitary fittings, railings suitable for the lake in the Public Park in Bikaner, and identify moulds for potato chips. M. Irigoin's work was just as arduous and included transacting the purchase of a property outside Paris, finding a golf instructor and an interpreter, arranging excursions 'through picturesque country', finding designs for cottages and following up with Hermès for an order of cigarette holders. Irigoin was also responsible for identifying the best French sculptor for making a portrait bust of the maharaja.

There were some shops which maharajas visited both to make purchases and because they were in themselves worth seeing. An example is found in London and Paris's palatial department stores, which excited considerable admiration among Indian visitors. One prince described Mr Whiteley, the founder of the eponymous shop in Bayswater the 'Napoleon of Commerce.'[102] In addition to stocking goods ranging from 'a pin to an elephant' emporia such as Whiteley's, The Army and Navy Stores and Harrods also provided a range of services, from catering weddings to arranging funerals. In the eyes of Francophile Jagatjit Singh of Kapurthala, Paris shops were far superior to those of London, particularly for the beauty with which they displayed wares.[103] So rich was the stock of French department store le Printemps 'that I found it

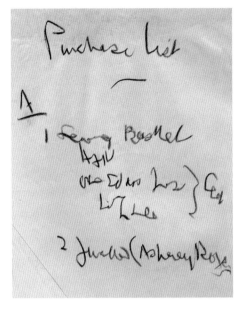

difficult to make a selection'. While in Paris, the maharaja made a point of calling into the principal luxury houses, among them Baccarat for glass-ware, Worth's for ladies' couture, and M. Pinaud's for perfumes and soaps. He took particular pleasure in visiting jewellers in Rue de la Paix. Porcelain factories and glassworks throughout Europe were regular stops for princes, who invariably needed articles for their new, substantially larger western-style palaces.[104] Maharajas were obvious targets for European tradesmen. Jagatjit Singh's prolific spending meant that 'Every day numbers of dealers call to exhibit their wares ... I have only to express a desire for something, a little different in pattern or design, and it is forthcoming immediately.'[105] Resisting was not always easy. Not ordinarily a great shopper, Sunity Devi of Cooch Behar nevertheless found that at Hamley's toy store 'I felt like buying the whole shop'.[106] The beautiful window displays in Naples cast such a spell over Jagatjit Singh that he found it difficult to 'resist purchasing the whole stock'.[107] As a child, Rajmata Gayatri Devi of Jaipur let her early passion for shopping run free. At the age of three she learned how to make her way from the family house in Knightsbridge to the Harrods toy department where, day after day, she made purchases which she masterfully put on account, until being found out![108]

Princes not only purchased from stock, but also commissioned works from the leading luxury houses. Some of their orders are the stuff of legend. The silver-encrusted bed ordered by Sadiq Muhammad Khan, Nawab of Bahawalpur (r. 1866-99) from Christofle in 1882 is a spectacular example of the encounter between western skill and Indian imagination (pp. 174-75). Maharaja Bhupinder Singh of Patiala's commissions from Cartier and Boucheron are dazzling episodes in the history of jewellery and reveal how princes appreciated western technical skill and styling, and how, in return, western jewellers admired the flamboyant Indian approach to using precious stones (pp. 68-69, 71-72 & 75-81). In automotive history, few stories can compete with those of maharajas and the fleets of vehicles they commissioned from leading car-makers (pp. 202-3). Some princes developed an eye for the best of western design. Maharaja Yeshwant Rao Holkar II of Indore (r. 1926-61) showed a budding interest in art from a young age and while only in his twenties commissioned avant-garde designers such as Le Corbusier, Ivan Da Silva Bruhns and Jean Puiforcat to create works for his Modernist palace Manik Bagh, a masterpiece of contemporary architecture designed by Eckart Muthesius (1904-89; pp. 268-69). Ranjitsinhji, Jam Saheb of Nawanagar (r. 1907-33) was renowned not only for his skills as a cricketer, but also for his superlative taste in jewels and in everything else (p. 86). Ranji 'was a lover of fine craftsmanship for its own sake, above all a lover of the modern' and 'never ceased to take delight in the perfection of all things around him, trivial or otherwise'.[109] The prince was a skilled designer himself, and invented improvements to all manner of practical goods, from chairs and tables to picnic baskets and travelling dressing tables. His design for a sliding cigarette case was taken up by Asprey's and put into production, with great success.

When added to the cost of their building projects and the expenses of their vast households, buying luxury goods from Europe invariably stretched the finances of Indian princes, many of whom owed substantial amounts to tradesmen in Europe.[110] An example may be found in the accounts of Bhupinder Singh of Patiala.[111] In 1930, when he appealed to the Government for a low-interest loan, the ruler owed more than £54,000 to European luxury houses (p. 74). His debtors included Garrard & Co., Holland & Holland, Thomas Cook & Sons, Osler & Co., Messrs Rolls-Royce & Co, Spink & Son, Messrs Alfred Dunhill, Messrs Henry Poole, and not unexpectedly, the firms of Cartier and Boucheron, both of whom had undertaken to reset the maharaja's vast collection of precious stones. Given his annual income of Rs 1,18,72,676 and his average expenditure of Rs 1,10,14,998, the maharaja found that without a loan he was simply unable to pay off his debts, which in total amounted to over Rs 1,92,85,750. The Government ultimately refused to advance a loan, but encouraged the maharaja to limit his privy purse to a reasonable percentage of his state's revenue. When the question arose of attending the coronation of George VI (r. 1937-52), the viceroy expressed his concern that, given the state of the Patiala finances, it would be imprudent for the maharaja to

24

Aldsworth, Surrey, was rented by Gaekwar Sayajirao III of Baroda in 1920 as a summer retreat in England. A few years later he acquired a residence in Paris, near the Parc Monceau.

Gaekwar Sayajirao III of Baroda and a guest playing boules at Aldsworth, 1920.

consider accepting the invitation.[112] Ultimately the ruler raised local loans to cover his outstanding bills.

Debts were not the only reason why, in the early 20th century, the Government began to express reluctance for some Indian princes to travel to the West. While in Europe, rulers enjoyed for the first time freedom from the constraints of court scrutiny. The West also offered them celebrity status; maharajas and their wives appeared in social columns in newspapers, and on the front of fashionable magazines. They mixed on equal terms with the aristocracy, with whom they shared mutual interests in racing and shooting. Some figures, like the dashing Aly Khan (1911-60), the amusing Brinda Devi of Kapurthala (for whom Cole Porter wrote *Let's Misbehave*) and the captivating Maharani Indira Devi of Cooch Behar were leading figures in the beau monde.[113] Mrs Evelyn Walsh recalls the impression created by Indira Devi in the casino at Le Touquet in the 1920s:[114]

> ...the most fabulously beautiful young Indian lady, holding the longest cigarette holder I had ever seen, wearing a brilliant silk sari and covered with pearls, emeralds and rubies. She was quite poker-faced but had a pile of chips in front of her to testify to her success and to top it all she had a little live turtle, whose back was laded with three strips of emeralds, diamonds, and rubies and which she was apparently using as a talisman. Every now and then the creature would crawl across the table but every time she caught it back. The crowd was totally mesmerised by her.

Maharajas found that, unlike in India, in Europe respect for their royal rank superseded any notion of racial prejudice. On easy terms with the British aristocracy and in some cases winning the particular friendship of the Royal Family, it was understandably galling for princes to return to India to be denied basic rights accorded to Europeans of inferior status. The pleasure of being in Europe meant that those rulers who could afford to, visited regularly and sometimes even bought houses in England and France in which to spend the summer. In doing so, princes were naturally away from their subjects more often, another major concern to the Government. Yeshwant Rao Holkar II of Indore was so frequently abroad that the Resident, K.S. Fitze proposed that the popular song *Some Day My Prince Will Come* be chosen as Indore's national anthem![115]

The West also offered another distraction in the form of free intercourse with the opposite sex. From the perspective of the Government, worse than mere fooling around was when princes decided to marry western women, a not infrequent occurrence.[116] Apart from blurring racial distinctions, such marriages invariably caused concern since the women were of inferior social background. In order to deal with these cases, the Government devised the policy that such women should 'neither lose or gain by her marriage'.[117] As such they were not allowed to assume the rank of their husbands and their children were denied rights of succession. In most instances this was not a concern since princes married European women only after having

25

produced a legitimate heir. However, Martanda of Pudukkottai married Molly Fink of Melbourne as his only wife. Their son was excluded from the succession and the ruler ultimately surrendered his throne and spent the rest of his days in Cannes.[118]

By the early 20th century the Government recognised that insolvency, detachment from social and political responsibility and compromising relationships were endemic among princes travelling regularly to Europe. In the eyes of Lord Curzon 'the result of European tours, particularly if too frequently repeated, is more often a collection of expensive furniture in the palace and of questionable proclivities in the mind of the returned traveller, than an increase in his capacity for public or political service.'[119] This was not always the case. For instance, in spite of his tendency to overspend, Jagatjit Singh of Kapurthala learnt much from his European tours and brought to his state innovations such as telephone and sewerage, reforms in administration and justice, as well as free public education. Nripendra Narayan of Cooch Behar, Ganga Singh of Bikaner, Ranjitsinhji of Nawanagar and Sayajirao III of Baroda likewise travelled extensively and introduced great improvements in their states, tackling invidious social injustices, promoting education and health care, developing communication networks, and, in the case of the latter, even establishing a museum in Baroda to bring to his people a taste of art from throughout Asia and the West.

As viceroy from 1899-1905, Lord Curzon issued a letter to the princes explaining that they required Government permission to travel abroad. Restrictions of this type made it clear that irrespective of the

visible symbols of authority granted to the princes, they possessed no sovereign rights. However, in some measure, British attitudes towards the princes changed with growing popular unrest in the early 20th century. The unpopular partition of Bengal in 1905, the largely unrecognised and unrewarded Indian contribution to the First World War, and the tragic 1919 Amritsar Massacre all created widespread disenchantment with British rule. Early 20th century calls for reform eventually led to a full-blown movement for self-rule. In the face of this crisis, the Government saw the maharajas as a force whose own interests dovetailed with those of the Empire. Various efforts were made to recognise the importance of the princes in the imperial order and it was even suggested that leading maharajas should be honoured with the title of king.[120] The fiercely loyal Maharaja Ganga Singh of Bikaner, who had made a considerable personal contribution during the First World War, was invited to represent India at the Peace Conference held at Versailles in 1919, and subsequently played a role in the League of Nations, as did Aga Khan III (1877-1957) and Ranjitsinhji, Jam Saheb of Nawanagar. In 1921 a new forum, the Chamber of Princes, was inaugurated as a way in which Indian rulers could formally voice their views and develop a concerted strategy in the changing political times. The Chamber was also meant to unite the princes and give them a common voice, although in reality leading states such as Hyderabad and Mysore largely chose to remain aloof from this body.

On one level, many princely families were sympathetic to the idea of self-rule; Gaekwar Sayajirao III of Baroda, for instance, was an early supporter of Indian nationalism and was celebrated for his belief in a free India. His granddaughter, Rajmata Gayatri Devi of Jaipur remembers how as a child 'we had supported the idea of independence, Mahatma Gandhi and Jawaharlal Nehru had been schoolroom heroes, and we often shouted Congress slogans about a free and united India.'[121] Maharaja Krishnaraja IV of Mysore (r. 1884-1940) likewise demonstrated his nationalism by following Mahatma Gandhi's (1869-1968) policy of *swadeshi* by taking up spinning. Princes were not always so easily reconciled with the driving forces of independence. Congress leaders in some cases considered princes to be little more than British ciphers; and maharajas by return were suspicious of Congress calls for responsible government within princely states. Even for princes who hoped for self-rule, the prospect of a free India was attended by great uncertainties about whether their

Nawab Sadiq Muhammed Khan Abbasi V of Bahawalpur, one of his European wives, and their entourage, at the Savoy Hotel, London, 1953. A visual comparison between the nawab and his grandfather (facing page) reflects a fundamental shift in the lifestyles of Indian princes under the Raj.

own rights and privileges would be secure once British paramountcy had lapsed. Interestingly, even after the Second World War some princes felt that their rule would continue as it had always done. In the words of Maharawal Lakshman Singh of Dungarpur (r. 1918-71): 'Nobody thought that princely rule would end at that time … Even in 1945 I never thought it would end.'[122]

Ultimately the advance of democracy was the undoing of princely India. In the rapidly changing times there was little room for an anachronistic form of government led by a group of maharajas who served little political purpose. With the guarantee of independence and Britain's hasty withdrawal from the subcontinent, each state was forced to merge into the new countries that emerged from the sadly partitioned subcontinent. A sense of unease is evident from the fact that

the rulers of Baroda, Gondal, Cutch, Jaipur, Faridkot and Indore all made efforts to take their jewellery out of India at this moment.[123] By the terms of the Indian instruments of accession, each prince was permitted to retain his private property and his personal privileges, but surrendered his political authority and his revenues in exchange for a privy purse income calculated at about ten per cent of his state's revenue.[124] Although deprived of political power, princes of course continued to retain their social position as leaders and as heads of clans; their dynastic heritage was clearly unaffected by the advent of democracy. Nevertheless, in the decades following Independence it was rarely possible for princely families to maintain their former way of life. Their incomes were simply too small to support the substantial palaces in which they lived. In her memoirs, Rajmata Gayatri Devi of Jaipur recalls the shock of learning in 1958 that her home, Rambagh Palace, was being turned into a hotel. Ultimately, her husband, Maharaja Man Singh II (r. 1922-70), 'insisted that I had to come to terms with the fact that, as long as the hotel guests paid their bills, they had as much right to be in the palace as I had.'[125]

Financial constraints on the royal houses tightened in 1971, when the Indian Government revoked the acts of parliament which guaranteed the rights of princes, depriving them of not only their titles and symbols of rank, but also their incomes. The change in the circumstances of maharajas over the past sixty years has brought about the dispersal of many princely collections. The fabulous jewels commissioned with aplomb in days of grandeur have been largely sold piecemeal at international auctions, or are in hiding, away from the attention of tax officials. The palaces built on a vast scale are now chiefly hotels or museums and their contents, paintings, libraries and chandeliers, cars and works of art have in some cases been sold to pay for expenses or to settle family disputes over inheritance. Still, the romance of princely Indian exists, evident, for instance, in the mesmerizing display arranged by Cartier in 2002 of the reconstructed Patiala diamond necklace (p. 75). Although set with cubic zirconium, this tour de force of jewellery, and the glamorous story behind it, captivated western audiences and brought to the fore the myth of the maharaja and the appeal of an age gone by.

27

THE ROYAL IMAGE

ᰍᰍᰍ

'WHEN THE PORTRAIT WAS FINISHED THE MAHARAJAH SAID
IT WAS LIKE LOOKING IN THE GLASS; AND THE MORNING I
LEFT, INSTEAD OF RECEIVING A CHEQUE AS I EXPECTED, A
LARGE SACK OF RUBIES WAS BROUGHT, SO HEAVY IT WAS
QUITE IMPOSSIBLE TO LIFT WITHOUT HELP.'

Emily Merrick, *With a Palette in Eastern Palaces*, 1899.

FACING PAGE: Nawab Sawar Ali Khan of Kurwai by Lafayette, c. 1922.

32

Nabob Omdut il Mulk.
Seragil Dowla Anaverden Caun.
Behauder Delaver Jung.
Nabob of Arcot, and the Carnatick.

King Ghazi-ud-din Haider of Oudh, oil on canvas. By Robert Home, c. 1820. The portrait depicts the ruler after the British Government elevated him to the rank of king in 1818. He wears a western-style pointed crown and an ermine cloak in the manner of a European monarch.

FACING PAGE: Nawab Muhammed Ali Wallajah of Arcot, oil on canvas. By Tilly Kettle, c. 1770. The ruler played an active role in the social life of the British community in Madras, adopting European habits and social conventions.

Nawab Shuja-ud-daula of Oudh and his ten sons, gouache on paper. By an Indian artist after a canvas by Tilly Kettle of 1772, c. 1815. The composition depicts the ruler and his sons being painted by a western artist, probably Tilly Kettle himself. The nawab commissioned a number of portraits from Kettle, one of which was sent as a diplomatic present to Louis XVI through the agencies of Jean-Baptiste Gentil, a Frenchman employed by the nawab to help reform his army.

FACING PAGE: Maharaja Sher Singh, oil on panel. By August Theodor Schoefft, 1845-50. The Hungarian-born artist based this portrait on a likeness made of the Sikh ruler during his stay in Lahore in 1841. The sitter was an aesthete and interested in the effects of western painting, commissioning Schoefft to produce a number of courtly portraits and landscapes. The Russian Prince Soltykoff described Sher Singh as 'a big stoutish man of forty, covered with the most beautiful jewels in the world'.

Princess Victoria Gouramma of Coorg, lithograph after an oil painting by Franz Xaver Winterhalter, 1852. Queen Victoria commissioned this portrait of the young sitter, who became her ward and favourite. Converted to Christianity in the private chapel at Buckingham Palace in a ceremony officiated by the Archbishop of Canterbury, the princess adopted the queen's name and was educated in the principles of the Church of England.

Maharaja Duleep Singh, oil on canvas. By Franz Xaver Winterhalter, 1854. This portrait of the dispossessed prince was commissioned by Queen Victoria, who visited the studio and noted how the artist 'was in ecstasies at the beauty and nobility of bearing of the young Maharajah. Winterhalter has got the whole figure beautifully.' Duleep Singh wears a portrait of the queen around his neck that was given to his father Maharaja Ranjit Singh by Lord Auckland, Governor-General of India from 1835 to 1842.

Maharaja Jitendra Narayan of Cooch Behar by Lafayette, 1913. The photograph of the young maharaja was taken in London shortly after his accession to the throne. The Eton-educated prince wears European shoes with his traditional *sherwani* (dress coat), and his turban is dressed with a platinum and diamond ornament probably made by a European jeweller. The ruler's mother (facing page) was herself photographed by Lafayette on several occasions.

FACING PAGE: Maharani Sunity Devi of Cooch Behar by Lafayette, 1902. The photograph was taken at the time of Edward VII's coronation. The sitter's gown and jewellery reflect her westernised tastes. The pearl and diamond badge with the letters VRI, Victoria Regina Imperatrix, belong to the Imperial Order of the Crown of India, founded in 1887 for women of the English royal family, wives of Indian princes and senior government officials in India.

40

Maharaja Ganga Singh of Bikaner, oil on canvas. By Sir William Orpen, 1919. Held in high esteem by the British Government, the maharaja was invited to participate at the Versailles Peace Conference in 1919, and was painted by Orpen, who was commissioned to produce portraits of statesmen attending the event. A contemporary observer felt that the maharaja 'was not only the archetype of an English gentleman but who spoke the English language in a way that was a lesson to all English men and women.'

FACING PAGE: Gaekwar Sayajirao III of Baroda by Lafayette, 1910. The second son of a village headman, Sayajirao was selected by the Government as heir to the throne and installed as gaekwar in 1875. Armed with a western education the ruler modernised Baroda by instituting social, economic and educational reforms. In this photograph Sayajirao poses for an equestrian portrait to be taken later that day. His uniform and badge are distinctive to Baroda, but modelled on western prototypes.

Gaekwar Sayajirao III of Baroda sitting for a portrait bust by an unidentified sculptor, 1927. The ruler was artistically inclined and patronised contemporary painters and sculptors to create works for Laxmi Vilas Palace. Sayajirao also admired Old Master paintings and formed a collection under the advice of Marion Harry Spielmann, Editor of the *Magazine of Art*.

73894 A.

24. 1. 81.

NB

Maharaj Dhiraj Patiala (grp 1).

5 dozen 12 x 10 Copies

This group to be entirely re-arranged
His Highness any position of single figure selected
No I. Her Highness from 73892 D. Jewels in nose vert - Sari.
No II. Her " " 73894 F. necklace to be partly covering
Jewels in nose foot of Sari.
& Daughters as in A. Jewels in nose.
Ladies in waiting, as in F. one lady
other one as in F. position,
A transparency afterwards please ⬭ 50.

44

Instructions for a photographic portrait of Maharaja Bhupinder Singh of Patiala and his family from the studio of Vandyk, 1931.

FACING PAGE: The family of Maharaja Bhupinder Singh of Patiala by Vandyk, 1931. Bhupinder Singh was a regular client of this photographer and invited him to Patiala to establish a studio and darkroom in Moti Bagh Palace.

47

Maharani Brinda Devi of Kapurthala, oil on canvas. By Philip de László (1869-1937).

FACING PAGE: Maharani Indira Devi of Cooch Behar, oil on canvas. By Philip de László (1869-1937).

The two western-educated princess were contemporaries and friends, Brinda naming her first daughter after Indira. Both women were active in European society in the inter-war period and were celebrated for their style and charm.

Maharani Gayatri Devi of Jaipur, c. 1955. The photographer captured the likeness of the celebrated princess in a dreamlike composition, her ethereal beauty matched by a

FACING PAGE: Rani Amrita Kaur of Mandi by Lafayette, 1924. The rani was photographed shortly before she was presented to George V and Queen Mary at Buckingham

FACING PAGE: Rani Sita Devi of Kapurthala attributed to Cecil Beaton, c. 1937. The setting reflects the contemporary appeal of white, a colour which enhances the impression of the princess's purity and youth, underlined by her sublime expression. The disembodied pose reflects Surrealist photography of the period.

Rani Sita Devi of Kapurthala, by André Durst, 1934. Durst accentuated the princess' beauty with pearls and rock crystal, both rare and precious substances. Although she regularly dressed in western clothes, in this photograph Sita Devi wears a sari that reflects her exotic origins. The image was published in *The Sketch* under the tile 'A Pearl of India'.

Maharaja Yeshwant Rao Holkar II of Indore in western dress, pencil on paper. By Bernard Boutet de Monvel, 1929. The ruler's engaging manner and his abiding interest in modern art won him the friendship of the artists and designers whom he commissioned. Among them was Bernard Boutet de Monvel, whom Indore commissioned to create portraits of himself and his family.

FACING PAGE: Maharaja Yeshwant Rao Holkar II of Indore in western dress, oil on canvas. By Bernard Boutet de Monvel, 1929. The portrait shows the prince at the age of twenty, shortly before he was invested with full ruling powers. His choice of dress reflects Yeshwant Rao's sophisticated western tastes.

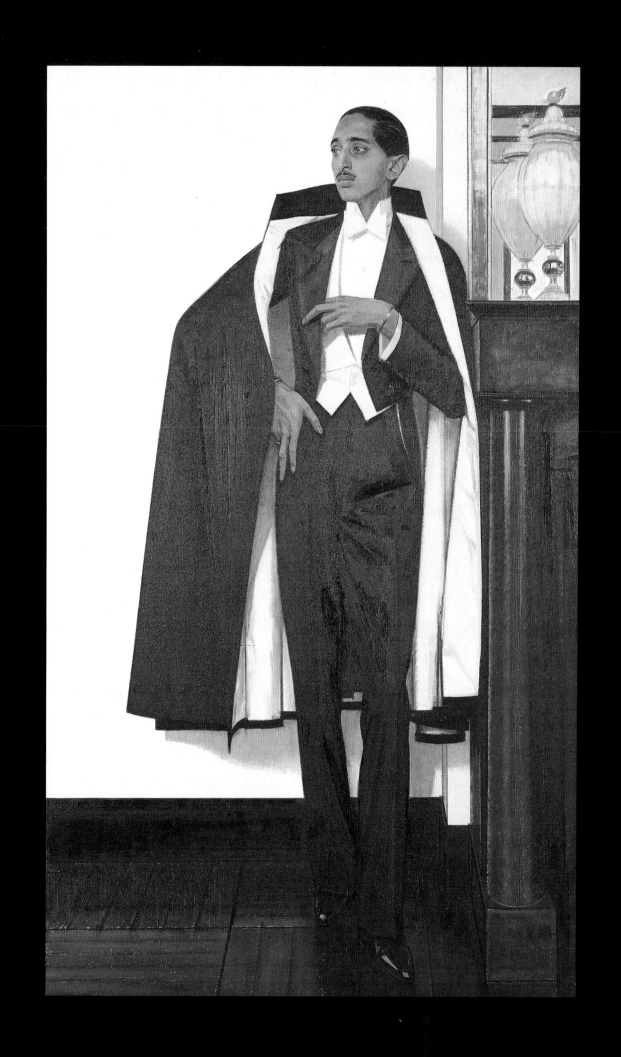

Maharanée d'Indore

55

FACING PAGE TOP LEFT: Maharaja Yeshwant Rao Holkar II of Indore, pencil on paper. By Bernard Boutet de Monvel, 1929.

FACING PAGE BOTTOM LEFT: Maharani Sanyogita of Indore, pencil on paper. By Bernard Boutet de Monvel, c. 1930.

FACING PAGE RIGHT: Maharaja Yeshwant Rao Holkar II of Indore in Maratha dress, pencil on paper. By Bernard Boutet de Monvel, c. 1934.

ABOVE: Maharaja Yeshwant Rao Holkar II of Indore in Maratha dress, oil on canvas. By Bernard Boutet de Monvel, 1934.

JEWELS

❧

'PRINCESS BRINDA OF KAPURTHALA, DAUGHTER-IN-LAW
OF THE MAHARAJA, HAD EVERY WOMAN GREEN WITH ENVY.
HER COLLECTION OF JEWELS WOULD MAKE TIFFANY AND
CARTIER TURN IN THEIR VAULTS. EMERALDS THE SIZE OF
WALNUTS HUNG FROM HER EARS AND DIAMOND
NECKLACES BY THE YARD CIRCLED HER THROAT.'

Vanity Fair, 1936.

FACING PAGE: Maharani Sita Devi of Baroda, by Henri Cartier-Bresson, 1948. Dressed for her husband's 40th birthday celebrations, Sita Devi wears an exceptional necklace which includes two celebrated Brazilian diamonds, the 128.8 carat Star of the South and the 78.53 carat English Dresden.

I n India precious stones are worn not only for their beauty, but also for their talismanic properties. In a royal context jewels played a further role as a reflection of the majesty of their owner and an indication of the richness of his treasury. To European observers the quantity of jewellery worn by Indian princes was a constant source of astonishment. The artist Valentine Prinsep (1838-1904), for example, was overwhelmed to see that in dressing Maharaja Tukoji Rao II of Indore (r. 1852-86) it took no less then six men, four of whom 'stand around with trays, on which are displayed jewels worth I do not know how many lacs'.[1] The artist Emily Merrick (b. 1842) found that Maharaja Rana Nihal Singh of Dholpur (r. 1873-1901) was 'a blaze of jewels' wearing £300,000 worth of treasure, of which he was exceptionally proud.[2] Yvonne Fitzroy (b. 1891) similarly observed that so richly jewelled was Maharaja Bhupinder Singh of Patiala (r. 1900-38) that 'his brocaded coat was entirely concealed by diamonds'.[3]

Indian princes were remarkably receptive to the work of European jewellers and eagerly commissioned them to reset their precious stones in the latest western styles. This represented a departure both in material and technique. The western preference for platinum and open claw settings replaced traditional gold jewellery with kundan work, in which stones were firmly set into a closed setting. The importance placed on jewellery by princes and their appreciation of western designs meant that they were ideal clients for European jewellers interested in expanding into overseas markets. By the second half of the 19th century a steady supply of western-made jewellery was already being sent to the subcontinent specifically for elite Indian consumers. Of both western and Indian form, these pieces were designed specifically to appeal to Indian tastes. In Calcutta the two leading retailers of this class of material were Hamilton & Co. and Garrard's.[4] While vicereine from 1884 to 1888, Harriet, Marchioness of Dufferin and Ava (1843-1936) visited what was probably one of these firms and recorded her observations: 'The jewels set in Europe for the eastern market are a curious mixture of splendour and childishness: watches encrusted with diamonds, and such complicated interiors that, besides telling you all you can possibly want to know about the time of the day or of the year, they play you a tune, and give you a representation of a conductor waving his baton as he sits somewhere on the face, mixed up with the seconds and the hours. Then there are ornaments for turbans, on which the diamond flowers, being wound up, whirl round and round till you can no longer see their shape.'[5] Indian princes were regular clients of European jewellers in India. For example, Asaf Jah VI, Nizam of Hyderabad (r. 1869-1911) and Bhupinder Singh of Patiala purchased jewellery from Calcutta and Madras firms such as Marcks & Co. Ltd; Lund, Blockley & Carter; Treacher & Co Ltd; Cooke & Kelvey, and the former ultimately appointed P. Orr and Sons his court jeweller.[6] These firms produced both western-style pieces and Indian forms such as *naths* (nose-rings), *bazubands* (armlets) and *payals* (anklets), although executed with European techniques.

Jewellery from western outlets in India was supplemented by pieces acquired by princes on their forays to Europe. Raja Rajaram of Kolhapur (r. 1866-70) was among the first princes to buy jewellery in Europe, recording in his dairy of 1870 a shopping trip to Bond Street where he 'Went to Hunt and Roskell's, where I bought some watches, earrings, &c.'[7] Princes also commissioned pieces. The Parisian firm of Cartier took the lead in soliciting orders. In 1909 the firm sent Jules Glaenzer and M. Prieur on a seven-month long speculative trip to the East to source pearls and precious stones and to establish links with potential clients. The pair enjoyed only limited success, but two years Jacques Cartier (1884-1942), head of the London branch, travelled to the subcontinent to further investigate the possibility of establishing relationships with Indian gem dealers and potential clients. Cartier's meetings with maharajas reveal that not only did they appreciate the aesthetic of contemporary European jewellery but that they were eager to reset their own stones in the latest western tastes.[8] For example, Gaekwar Sayajirao III of Baroda (r. 1875-1939) entrusted Cartier with the task of reworking all of his jewellery into platinum, but local jewellers from Baroda who resented the young Frenchman's influence ultimately prevented him from proceeding with the job.[9] Cartier was not the only firm to enjoy the Gaekwar's patronage. For the engagement in 1911 of his daughter Indira Devi (1892-1968) to Maharaja Madho Rao Scindia of Gwalior (r. 1886-1925), he purchased jewellery from the Parisian firm Chaumet and records indicate that in the same period he was also buying stock items from Boucheron.[10] When she travelled to the West, the Gaekwar's wife, Chimnabai II (1872-1958), took her jeweller with her to advise on her purchases from European firms.[11]

Cartier's archives reveal that, as was the case with other luxury goods, selling jewellery to Indian princes was occasionally a long and complex affair. Transactions were sometimes conducted in London and Paris, but most often it was the Company's agents in India who executed orders, undertaking to visit rulers, to supply them with designs and models from Europe for their approval, to take charge of their precious stones and to collect payments. Commissioning jewellery at such a distance was not always easy, as is indicated by an order given by Sayajirao III of Baroda to Cartier in 1928 for three pairs of diamond bracelets. In spite of extensive correspondence and the use of models (the first set of which were damaged in transit), the bracelets were the wrong size and had to be made again.[12] As was the case with the furnishers Maple & Co., Cartier's local agents approached royal families who were celebrating marriages and jubilees, hoping to secure business from them at a time of high spending. Cartier's forays into the Indian market were not only to find clients, but also to source precious stones and to purchase from local dealers old and new Indian jewellery, which they resold in Europe.[13] Exposure to Indian jewellery ultimately inspired the firm's own eastern-style creations; just as maharajas admired western settings in platinum, so did western clients develop a penchant for the decorative effects of Indian jewellery, particularly the flamboyant mixture of coloured stones, marketed under the label 'tutti frutti', and the effect of multi-stranded ropes and tassels of pearls and jewels.

Although numerous commissions were executed by European jewellers for Indian princes, it is invariably the most spectacular that are remembered. Among these is a celebrated emerald turban ornament made by Cartier's Paris workshop in 1926 for Jagatjit Singh, Maharaja of Kapurthala (r. 1877-1949; p. 65). The ruler was highly westernised, spent as much time as possible in France, spoke fluent French, and married European women as his fifth and sixth wives. As is evident from his diary, he was a keen shopper and from his first trip to Europe admired the work of European jewellers. For example, he spent the morning of 12 June 1893 'in visiting jewellers and the shops in the Rue de la Paix, a very attractive street'.[14] The Cartier turban ornament, commissioned in time for the ruler's Golden Jubilee, was not his first order from a Parisian jeweller; in 1905 he had asked Boucheron to create a turban ornament with diamonds which he supplied from his treasury (p. 65).[15] But such commissions pale in significance compared to the jewels reset by Parisian jeweller Boucheron for Bhupinder Singh of Patiala during his visit to Paris in 1928 (pp. 68-69, 71 & 80-85). Baron Fouquier recorded how in 1928 the ruler causes a sensation in Paris with his retinue of forty servants.[16] Among his luggage were six iron chests of precious stones, which were sent to Louis Boucheron (1874-1959), whom the maharaja had met in 1926, while the jeweller was in India scouting for business. As well as numerous sapphires, rubies and pearls, the collection included over seven thousand diamonds

and more than fourteen hundred emeralds. These were worked into one hundred and forty-nine pieces of jewellery. Among them were traditional designs such as *bazubands* (armlets) and *sarpeches* (turban ornaments) as well as more universal forms such as necklaces and earrings, all designed with clear Indian references, but executed in an Art Deco taste. According to Fouquier, Patiala was so delighted by Boucheron's jewellery that to mark the occasion he gave a party to which were invited the community of Indian princes passing through Paris at the time.

Louis Boucheron must have been surprised to learn soon after he had received the maharaja of Patiala's order that Cartier was staging an exhibition at Rue de la Paix of 'Crown Jewels' which they had reset for the same prince! This substantial order had been placed in 1925 and likewise included a variety of forms, both Indian and western. Among the pieces were two enormous diamond necklaces. The first consisted of three strands of large uncut diamonds embellished with diamond pendants. The second consisted of five strands of substantial diamonds, with the light yellow 234.69 carat De Beers diamond as its central pendant (p. 75). The exhibition was an instant success. In the words of a contemporary writer, 'At Cartier's dreams take shape, we are in the world of One Thousand and One Nights, and the beauty, and the extent of his collection surpasses the imagination.'[17] In quantitative terms the Patiala order is the largest single commission that Cartier has ever executed, although in value the firm clearly made greater profits when supplying stones as well as settings. Information about the Patiala's accounts indicate that Bhupinder Singh was financially stretched; by

59

Label from an album of drawings and photographs of jewellery made by Boucheron for Maharaja Bhupinder Singh of Patiala, 1928.

1930 he had not yet paid Boucheron and Cartier and was petitioning the Government for a loan in order to settle his enormous debts.[18] The accounts must have been settled without much further delay as Cartier accepted another order to reset a substantial number of the maharaja's stones in 1935.

Cartier was also central in forming the jewellery collection of Ranjitsinhji, Jam Saheb of Nawanagar (r. 1907-33). The ruler had been educated at Trinity College, Cambridge, and attained world-wide fame as a champion batsman for the All-England team, winning the affectionate nickname 'the Black Prince of cricketers'. A lover of the English way of life, Ranji nevertheless understood that the possession of great jewels was an integral aspect of Indian kingship and with this in mind, on his accession to the throne he set about enriching the Nawanagar treasury. Over the course of his life Ranji developed a keen appreciation of jewellery and was regarded internationally as an authority on precious stones. His biographer reveals that 'Like many collectors, he was terrifyingly casual in the care of his jewels. He travelled with several suitcases full of rings, watches and ornaments, besides the most important items in the State collection.'[19] In his rooms 'Drawers and wardrobes were full of pieces of jewellery, apparently lying haphazard, but in reality carefully card-indexed both in his own mind and that of his servant, who followed him everywhere for thirty-seven years with the devotion of a spaniel.'

The jam saheb acquired the renowned 136.25 carat cushion-shaped Queen of Holland diamond (later re-cut to 135.92 carats), renamed the Ranjitsinhji, and asked Jacques Cartier to mount it for him in a spectacular multi-stranded necklace composed of an exceptional group of white and coloured diamonds. The prince also commissioned from Cartier a fine emerald and diamond necklace

Publicity material for an exhibition which Cartier staged in Paris to display jewellery designed by the firm for Maharaja Bhupinder Singh of Patiala, 1928.

with matching turban ornament (p. 86). Both pieces were conceived in an angular Art Deco style, the necklace with a recently-acquired 70-carat emerald and the turban ornament with an emerald of 40 carats 'remarkable for its fire'.[20] Ranji's taste in settings was determined above all by his fascination with the stones themselves, a subject in which he developed considerable expertise. In this skill he was assisted by an exceptional memory and an innate understanding of the attributes sought after in a fine jewel. Ranji's successor Digvijaysinhji (r. 1933-66) continued this relationship with Cartier, commissioning in 1937 an extraordinary necklace to show off a total of 118 rubies from the Nawanagar treasury (p. 87). The firm also supplied him with a remarkable 61.50 carat whisky-coloured diamond, which Cartier set in 1937 as a turban ornament that could be converted into a broach.'[21]

The princely house of Indore also made substantial purchases of jewellery through European firms. Before the First World War, Maharaja Tukoji Rao Holkar III (r. 1903-26) bought from Chaumet a pair of exceptional pear-shaped Golconda diamonds, subsequently known as the 'Indore Pears' (pp. 66 & 94-5). When his successor Maharaja Yeshwant Rao II (r. 1926-61) was invested with full ruling powers in 1930, he too began buying jewellery, but turned to the Parisian firm of Mauboussin, which sold the prince the 56.40 carat Porter Rhodes diamond in 1937. Yeshwant Rao's loyalty to Mauboussin was partly inspired by his close friendship with employee Jean Goulet, who was the same age as the prince and shared his interest in Indian religions. He appointed the firm his official jewellers and invited Goulet to Indore to catalogue and appraise the treasury, a task which took two months to complete. Among the works commissioned from Mauboussin were a *sarpech* (turban ornament) and *turra* (turban tassel), both of traditional form, but set in platinum and fashioned in a distinctly Deco idiom (p. 66). The firm provided the prince with a number of pieces of jewellery and suggested various designs for the Indore Pears, setting these spectacular diamonds into a necklace in 1937. The prince's orders could not have come at a better time; the collapse of Wall Street in 1929 led to a period of economic depression and with it a downturn in the demand for luxury goods. At this time Indian princes were critical in sustaining luxury houses.

Following the independence of India in 1947 few maharajas were able to keep their treasuries intact.[22] As easily disposable assets, jewels were among the first possessions that princes sold in the face of financial pressure. From the 1950s onwards, European jewellers travelling to India were typically not selling, but acquiring precious stones from maharajas, and selling them to advantage in Europe or America. The account written by Claude Arpels (1911-90) following a visit to India in 1956 to purchase jewels captures this poignant age. At Rewah, Maharaja Martand Singh (r. 1946-72) received the jeweller and laid out for him in a palace courtyard a vast array of jewels from which to make a selection. As Arpels noted, the moment 'was not without pathos, reflected in the eyes of His Highness who seemed to be living for a few moments in the glamorous past.'[23] Among the pieces he chose to buy were 'a garland of large diamonds of every known, shape', a necklace 'of 56 emeralds fringed with diamonds and hundreds of beautiful oriental pearls. At the centre, hangs a wondrous emerald pendant, solid gold bangles, some studded with large diamonds, and a host of precious stones and carved jade daggers.'

Among the few princes who commissioned significant works from European jewellers after Independence were Aga Khan III (r. 1885-1957) and Gaekwar Pratapsinhrao of Baroda (r. 1939-51) and his second wife, Sita Devi (1917-86), a passionate collector of jewellery (p. 56). The Gaekwar's ancestors had formed a legendary collection of jewels that included a set of exceptional pearls and

famous diamonds such as the 128.80 carat Star of the South and the 78.53 carat English Dresden. These two stones were mounted in a single, extraordinary necklace. French traveller Louis Rousselet had the opportunity to wear this piece when touring the Baroda treasury in the 1870s, noting how 'I felt crushed beneath the enormous weight of these jewels'.[24] In the thirteen years she was married to the Gaekwar, Sita Devi is believed to have sold or had many of Baroda's finest jewels reset, principally by Van Cleef &

As well as working for Indian princes Cartier also purchased old and new Indian jewellery which they retailed to their clients in Europe and America. This invitation of 1912 asks customers in London to visit a sale of pieces recently acquired by the firm in India.

Arpels (pp. 88-89).[25] Among the stories associated with her is that of a pair of exceptional emerald and diamond anklets which she sold to Harry Winston in 1953. The jeweller transformed these into a necklace for the Duchess of Windsor, who wore the piece to a New York party attended by Sita Devi. Hearing the praise for the duchess's necklace, Sita Devi retorted that the jewels had also looked good when she had worn them on her feet! Needless to say, the duchess returned the necklace and Winston had to find another buyer.

Yuvaraj Kanthirava Narasimharaja Wodeyar of Mysore by Lafayette, 1920. The sitter is the second son of Maharaja Jayachamarajndra of Mysore and in his turban wears a diamond double-headed eagle (*gandabherunda*), the symbol of the Wodeyar dynasty. He is dressed with the sash and star of a Knight Grand Commander of the Most Eminent Order of the Indian Empire. The diamond jewellery is European and set in platinum.

FOR THE BROW OF A GREAT PRINCE

A Cartier creation for the Maharajah of Kapurthala, who is known for his excellent taste. One of the most enlightened of Hindu princes, he spends a part of each year in Paris. He is such an admirer of French architecture that he had a French architect go to India to build him a Louis XVI palace

The Maharajah, like most of the other Indian potentates, has faith in the increasing value of pearls and precious stones and regularly devotes a portion of his annual income to increasing his collection. The Hindu princes look upon gems as a permanent investment to pass from generation to generation

ABOVE: Advertisement from *The Spur*, 1926. Cartier's prestige was much enhanced by the extraordinary jewellery they created for Indian princes. This advertisement from the firm impresses readers with the aesthetic and financial importance of the Kapurthala commission.

LEFT: Turban ornament, platinum set with diamonds. Made for Maharaja Jagatjit Singh of Kapurthala by Boucheron, 1905. The ruler was a regular visitor to Paris and an early client of Boucheron, asking the firm to create this piece from diamonds he supplied.

BELOW RIGHT: Turban ornament, platinum set with emeralds, diamonds and pearls. Made for Maharaja Jagatjit Singh of Kapurthala by Cartier, 1926. The ruler commissioned the headdress in time for his Golden Jubilee. The precious stones came from his treasury, among them the central flat hexagonal emerald of 177 carats.

FACING PAGE: Maharaja Jagatjit Singh of Kapurthala by G.L. Manuel Frères, c. 1930. The ruler wears the emerald turban ornament created for him by Cartier in 1926.

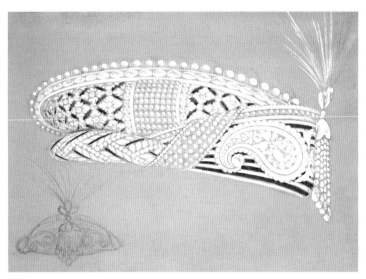

TOP: Design for a Maratha-style turban with pearls, emeralds and diamonds; watercolour and gouache on paper. By Joseph Chaumet, probably for Maharaja Tukoji Rao Holkar III of Indore, c. 1920.

BOTTOM: Design for a turban ornament and jewel with diamonds; watercolour and gouache on paper. By Joseph Chaumet, c. 1910. The style of turban suggests that this commission was intended for a Sikh prince.

TOP: Model for a *sarpech* (turban ornament) with diamonds and emeralds; gouache on lead. Made by Mauboussin for Maharaja Yeshwant Rao Holkar II of Indore, 1935. The design incorporates the Indore Pears, two sensational pear-shaped diamonds acquired by Maharaja Tukoji Rao Holkar III from Chaumet in the early 1910s.

BOTTOM: *Sarpech* and *turra* (turban tassel), platinum, set with diamonds and emeralds. Made by Mauboussin for Yeshwant Rao Holkar II of Indore, 1936. The ornament is the realisation of a lead model (above), excluding the Indore Pears.

FACING PAGE: Maharaja Ghanshyamsinhji of Dhranghadra wearing a turban ornament made by Cartier in 1935. The central emerald is 160 carats.

Bazuband (armlet), platinum, set with diamonds and emeralds. Made by Boucheron for Maharaja Bhupinder Singh of Patiala, 1928.

FACING PAGE: Three designs for *bazubands*, platinum, set with diamonds, emeralds and various precious stones; gouache on paper. By Boucheron for Maharaja Bhupinder Singh of Patiala, 1928.

Under the patronage of maharajas leading European jewellers applied their skills to producing jewellery in traditional Indian forms. These designs were part of an extensive commission given to Boucheron by Maharaja Bhupinder Singh of Patiala in 1928.

71

FACING PAGE: Maharani Bakhtavar Kaur of Patiala, c. 1920. This painted photograph depicts the senior wife of Maharaja Bhupinder Singh of Patiala.

TOP LEFT: Design for a forehead ornament, platinum with diamonds, pearls and emeralds; gouache on paper. By Boucheron for Maharaja Bhupinder Singh of Patiala, 1928.

TOP RIGHT: Forehead ornament, platinum with diamonds, pearls and rubies. Made by Boucheron for Maharaja Bhupinder Singh of Patiala, 1928.

BOTTOM: *Nath* (nose-ring), platinum, diamonds and pearls. Supplied by Cartier to Maharaja Bhupinder Singh of Patiala, 1928. Cartier sometimes used independent Parisian workshops on a contractual basis. This piece was executed for the firm by the atelier of Henri Lavabre.

LEFT: Maharaja Rajinder Singh of Patiala, c. 1890. Government regulations prohibited Indian princes from wearing western-style crowns. In order to overcome this stricture, some princes simply wore tiaras over their turbans, thereby simulating the effect of a crown without crossing official policy.

CENTRE: The Patiala Necklace, platinum set with diamonds and rubies; photograph overpainted with gouache and ink. By Cartier for Maharaja Bhupinder Singh of Patiala, 1928. This image provides a schematic view of the extraordinary five-stranded platinum bib necklace made for the maharaja by Cartier. The necklace was mounted with 2,930 diamonds.

RIGHT: Maharaja Bhupinder Singh of Patiala, early 20th century. The ruler succeeded to the throne at the age of nine, and was only invested with full powers in 1909, at the age of eighteen.

FACING PAGE: Maharaja Bhupinder Singh of Patiala by Vandyk, 1911. This formidable portrait conveys a sense of the ruler's appetite for precious stones. In 1925 he decided to reset a large number of the Patiala jewels, giving Cartier what is in quantitative terms the most substantial commission the firm has ever received. Only three years later he supplied Boucheron with yet another extensive collection of stones, which was transformed into 149 pieces of jewellery.

Detail of cheques payable to foreign firms.

. Count Jean De Madre, Paris   £.   343-14--0

. Messrs. Chas J. Sawyer Ltd., London.   4--9--0

   Messrs Peal & Co., London.   59-14--6

                     Total   £.   407-17--6

#	Firm		Amount
4.	Messrs Spink & Son, London	Rs.	1,21,666--0--9
5.	Messrs Vandyk Ltd., London.	£.	858-17--3
6.	do do	£.	7,000--0--0
7.	Messrs Tronchil, Paris	£	1,000--0--0
8.	Messrs Thomas Cook & Son, Bombay.	£	1,081-11-11
9.	(European Firm) ?	£	113-6--7
10.	Messrs Spink & Sons Ltd., London.	£	17,777-13--6
11.	Messrs Alred Dunhill.	£	583--0--0
12.	do (£.545)	Rs.	7,630--0--0
13.	Messrs Goldsmiths & Silversmiths, ~~Regent Str~~, London.	£.	1,217-17--6
14.	Messrs Barella, Berlin	£.	790-10--4
15.	Messrs Atliers Ltd., ~~96, Warder St.~~, London.	£.	522-19--6
16.	Messrs Finnagans Ltd., ~~New Bond St.~~ London	£.	350-15--0
17.	Messrs Theodre Hamblin Ltd., ~~15 Bigmore~~ St. Avendish, ~~Sq.~~ London. ~~W.1~~	£.	357--0--0
18.	Messrs Cartier	£.	6,921--8--0
19.	do (£ 338/14/)	Rs.	4,573--0--0
20.	Messrs Bonchern	£.	12,323--2--0
21.	do (£.58/-)	Rs.	783--0--0
22.	Messrs Barcley, Paris	£.	1,560--0--0
23.	Messrs Henary Pool, Paris	£.	1,441-15--6
24.	Messrs Jean Masonaiane, France.	Frk	1,880

                   Total   Rs. 1,34,652--0--9

                               £   54,307-14--2

Amounts owed by Maharaja Bhupinder Singh of Patiala to foreign firms, 1930. The maharaja applied to the Government for a low-interest loan in order to pay off his debts. Among the firms to which he owed funds were Cartier and Boucheron, who had recently reset some of the prince's jewels. He also owed funds to Garrards, Holland & Holland, Thomas Cook, F&C Osler and Rolls-Royce. The ruler paid off these bills with loans secured from local moneylenders.

The Patiala Necklace, platinum set with diamonds, white topazes, synthetic rubies, a smokey quartz, a citrine, white zirconias and a yellow zirconia. Made by Cartier for Maharaja Bhupinder Singh of Patiala, 1928; reset with substitute stones, 2002. This extraordinary ceremonial piece originally displayed a rich selection of the Patiala diamonds, amounting to 962.25 carats. The central pendant solitaire is the light yellow 234.65 carat De Beers diamond, exhibited at the Exposition Universelle in Paris, 1889 and purchased by Maharaja Rajinder Singh of Patiala shortly thereafter. The necklace mysteriously disappeared and resurfaced in a London jewellery store in 1998, the majority of its stones missing. Cartier purchased it and reconstructed the piece using substitute stones, displaying it to great acclaim in 2002.

FACING PAGE: Maharaja Bhupinder Singh of Patiala with ladies of his family, by Vandyk, 1931. One of the ruler's wives (seated left) wears the dramatic ruby necklace shown above.

Necklace, platinum set with rubies, diamonds and pearls. Made by Cartier for Maharaja Bhupinder Singh of Patiala, 1928.

78

Necklace, platinum, set with emeralds. Made by
Cartier for Maharaja Bhupinder Singh of Patiala, 1928.

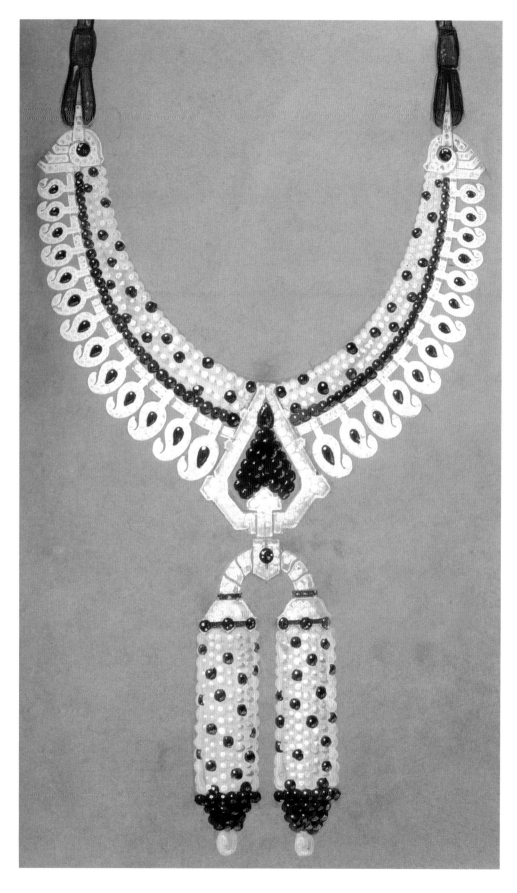

Design for a necklace, platinum with diamonds, pearls and rubies; pencil and watercolour on paper. Supplied by Cartier to Maharaja Bhupinder Singh of Patiala, 1935. In 1935 the maharaja commissioned Cartier to set a number of his precious stones. This piece, made for the firm by the workshop of Henri Lavabre, consisted of 834 diamonds, 1,159 pearls and 355 rubies.

VIII.

FACING PAGE: Design for a necklace, platinum with rubies, pearls, emeralds and diamonds; gouache on paper. By Boucheron for Maharaja Bhupinder Singh of Patiala, 1928.

Necklace, platinum with rubies, pearls, emeralds and diamonds. Made by Boucheron for Maharaja Bhupinder Singh of Patiala, 1928.

3205 R.P. Exportation Nº 1369.

S.A. Maharaja Dhiraj of Patiala   London

96 Reçu :

1 Un lot de : 1432 Émeraudes

349 sur papier pesant : 7799 cts 73.

2 Un lot de 2636 Brillants pesant
ensemble : 354 cts 76 s/ papier.

Fourni 3 Un lot de 4935 Brillants pesant : 211c 88
provenant du démonté des montures
des brillants tables de notre Dº.

Reçu : 13 Perles de collier grises 1999 gr 63

5 Un collier fleurs rubis clairs
et brillants plats.

6 Un lot de rubis taillés pesant : 641 c 65
sur papier.

7 Un lot de rubis de mauvaise
qualité, percés cabochons pesant :

8 Un pendentif feuilles émeraudes
gravées et roses.

9 Un grand ornement de turban
en or et émeraudes très claires
dont 3 grandes pierres manquent.

	Magasin : 31 Oct.	.	s x x
	" 8 hoo.	.	s 2h x
	" 9 hov.	.	2 x
	" 12 hov.	.	a x
	Jugla et Cº 12 hov.	.	2h x
	13 hov.	.	sa x
	Barreau : 20.11.28	.	8 6 x x
	" 20.11.28	.	hh x
	" 20.11.28	.	ss x x x
	" 29.11.28	.	6 o t
	" 29.11.28	.	t h t
	atelier 20 hov.	.	t h r
	Bruneau 28 hov.	.	nh r
	Moy. schelgy 23 hoo.	.	sh ht x
	du nº 3550.	.	s b a t
	Reporté :		i h a o h

INSET: Jewellers from Boucheron in India negotiating with local traders, early 20th century. European jewellers visited India not only to solicit business but also to purchase pearls and precious stones. On his 1926 Indian tour Louis Boucheron visited Maharaja Bhupinder Singh of Patiala, who at the time purchased only a few minor items in gold. Two years later the ruler arrived at Boucheron's showroom in Place Vendome, Paris, and placed a substantial order, bringing with him a rich collection of jewels to be reset.

Boucheron ledger itemising work undertaken for Maharaja Bhupinder Singh of Patiala, 1928.

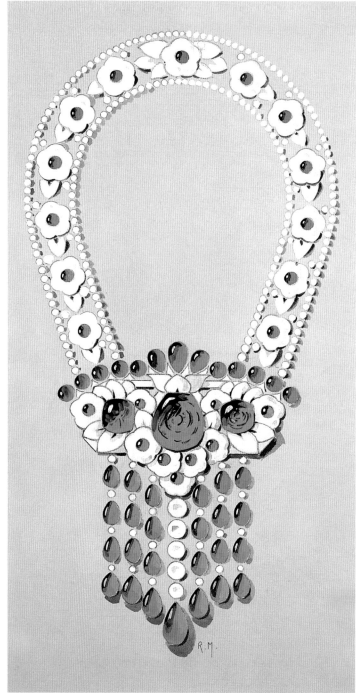

Design for a necklace, platinum with emeralds, diamonds and rubies; gouache on paper. By Boucheron for Maharaja Bhupinder Singh of Patiala, 1928. The completed necklace contained 118 emeralds (1,496.03 carats), 800 diamonds (57.23 carats) and 43 rubies (245.65 carats).

Design for a necklace, platinum with emeralds, diamonds and pearls; gouache on paper. By Boucheron for Maharaja Bhupinder Singh of Patiala, 1928.

Necklace, platinum with emeralds and diamonds. Made by Boucheron for Maharaja Bhupinder Singh of Patiala, 1928. The necklace is composed of 85 emeralds (1,117.25 carats) and 1,369 diamonds (124.48 carats).

LEFT: Design for a necklace, platinum with emeralds and diamonds; gouache on paper. By Boucheron for Maharaja Bhupinder Singh of Patiala, 1928.

Design for a necklace, platinum with emeralds and diamonds; gouache on paper. By Boucheron for Maharaja Bhupinder Singh of Patiala, 1928.

Design for a necklace, platinum with emeralds and diamonds; gouache on paper. By Boucheron for Maharaja Bhupinder Singh of Patiala, 1928.

Jam Saheb Ranjitsinhji of Nawanagar by Lafayette, 1920. Ranji was both a renowned cricketer and a collector of jewels. Jacques Cartier considered his emeralds 'unequalled in the world, if not in quantity, then in quality'. The prince was himself a connoisseur of precious stones: 'Dealers came to see him from all over the world, and his offers were quoted as a criterion on which future transactions should be based.' In this portrait Ranji is dressed as for a reception given by George V in London on the following day. In addition to his jewellery, he wears the Star of a Knight Grand Cross of the Most Excellent Order of the British Empire.

Necklace, platinum with emeralds and diamonds. Made by Cartier for Jam Saheb Ranjitsinhji of Nawanagar, 1926. The necklace is composed of seventeen emeralds, the central pendant weighing 70 carats alone. It was accompanied by a *sarpech* with an emerald of 39.43 carats.

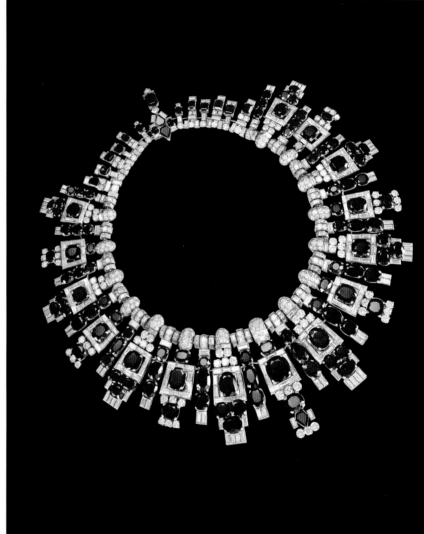

Jam Saheb Digvijaysinhji of Nawanagar, c. 1935. The ruler wears a collar and a necklace both of emeralds and diamonds set for his predecessor Ranjitsinhji by Cartier.

Necklace, platinum with rubies and diamonds. Made by Cartier for Jam Saheb Digvijaysinhji of Nawanagar, 1937. Cartier produced this piece using 116 rare Burmese rubies from the Nawanagar treasury, providing the diamonds themselves. In the early 1950s the necklace was returned to Cartier for resale.

TOP LEFT: Design for a necklace, platinum with diamonds and emeralds; gouache and pencil on paper. By Van Cleef & Arpels for Maharani Sita Devi of Baroda, 1949.

TOP RIGHT: Jacques Arpels and his daughter Dominique Hourtoulle studying an image of the necklace created for Maharani Sita Devi in 1949-50, 1983.

LEFT AND ABOVE: Necklace and pair of earrings, platinum with diamonds and emeralds. Made by Van Cleef & Arpels for Maharani Sita Devi of Baroda, 1949-50. The jewellery was resold by Sita Devi in 1974.

FACING PAGE: Maharani Sita Devi of Baroda with her son Sayajirao Gaekwar, 1948.

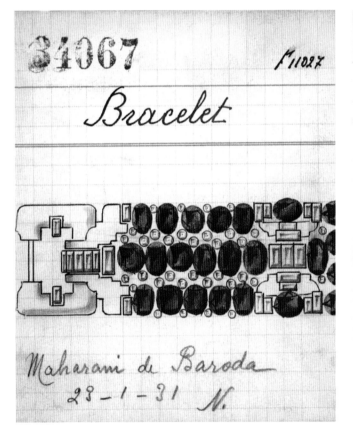

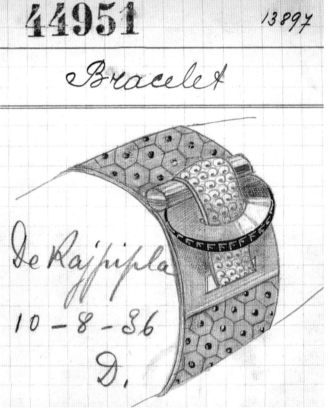

The Van Cleef & Arpels archives reveal that Indian princes were the firm's regular clients, both for stock items and special commissions.

TOP: Design for a bracelet, platinum with diamonds; gouache and pencil on paper. Made by Van Cleef & Arpels for Maharani Sita Devi of Baroda, 1950. This piece was commissioned by Sita Devi under the pseudonym Mrs Brown.

BOTTOM: Design for a bracelet, platinum with diamonds and rubies; gouache and pencil on card. Made by Van Cleef & Arpels and purchased by Maharani Chimnabai II of Baroda, 1931.

TOP: Design for a bracelet, platinum with five rows of pearls, diamonds, and an emerald; gouache and pencil on paper. Made by Van Cleef & Arpels for Maharani Sita Devi of Baroda, 1950.

BOTTOM: Design for a bracelet, gold with rubies and diamonds; gouache and ink on card. Made by Van Cleef & Arpels and purchased by Maharaja Vijaysinhji Chhatrasinhji of Rajpipla, 1936.

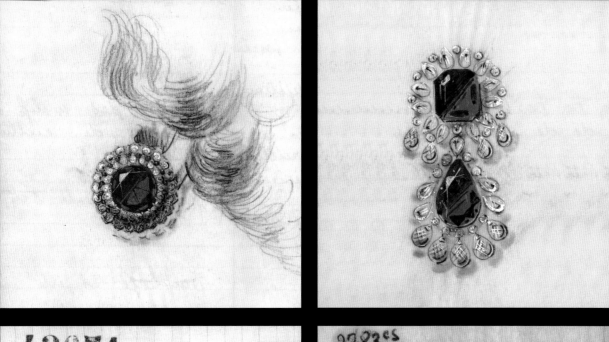

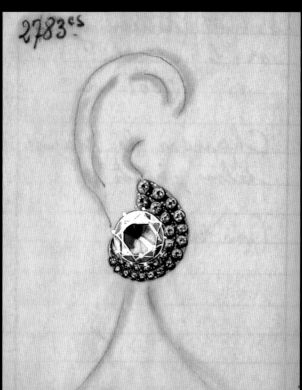

TOP: Design for earrings, platinum with emeralds; gouache and pencil on paper. Made by Van Cleef & Arpels for Maharani Sita Devi of Baroda, 1950. This piece was commissioned by Sita Devi under the pseudonym Mrs Brown.

BOTTOM: Design for earrings, platinum with diamonds and sapphires; gouache and pencil on card. Made by Van Cleef & Arpels and purchased by a princess from Kapurthala, 1935.

TOP: Design for earrings, platinum with emeralds; gouache and pencil on paper. Made by Van Cleef & Arpels for Maharani Sita Devi of Baroda, 1950.

BOTTOM: Design for earrings, gold with diamonds; gouache and pencil on paper. Made by Van Cleef & Arpels for Maharani Sita Devi of Baroda, 1952.

92

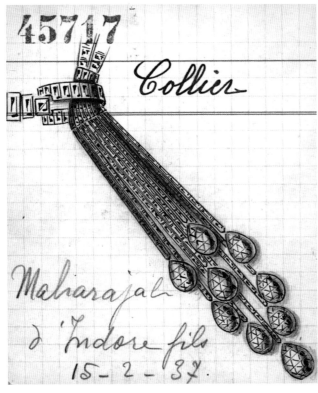

TOP: Design for a pendant, platinum with diamonds; gouache and ink on card. Made by Van Cleef & Arpels and purchased by Gaekwar Sayajirao III of Baroda, 1928.

BOTTOM: Design for a necklace, platinum with diamonds; gouache and ink on card. Made by Van Cleef & Arpels and purchased by Maharaja Yeshwant Rao Holkar II of Indore, 1937.

TOP: Design for a clip, platinum set with diamonds; gouache on card. Made by Van Cleef & Arpels and purchased by Maharaja Man Singh II of Jaipur, 1937.

BOTTOM: Broach, platinum set with diamonds and pearls. Made by Boucheron for Maharaja Bhupinder Singh of Patiala, 1928.

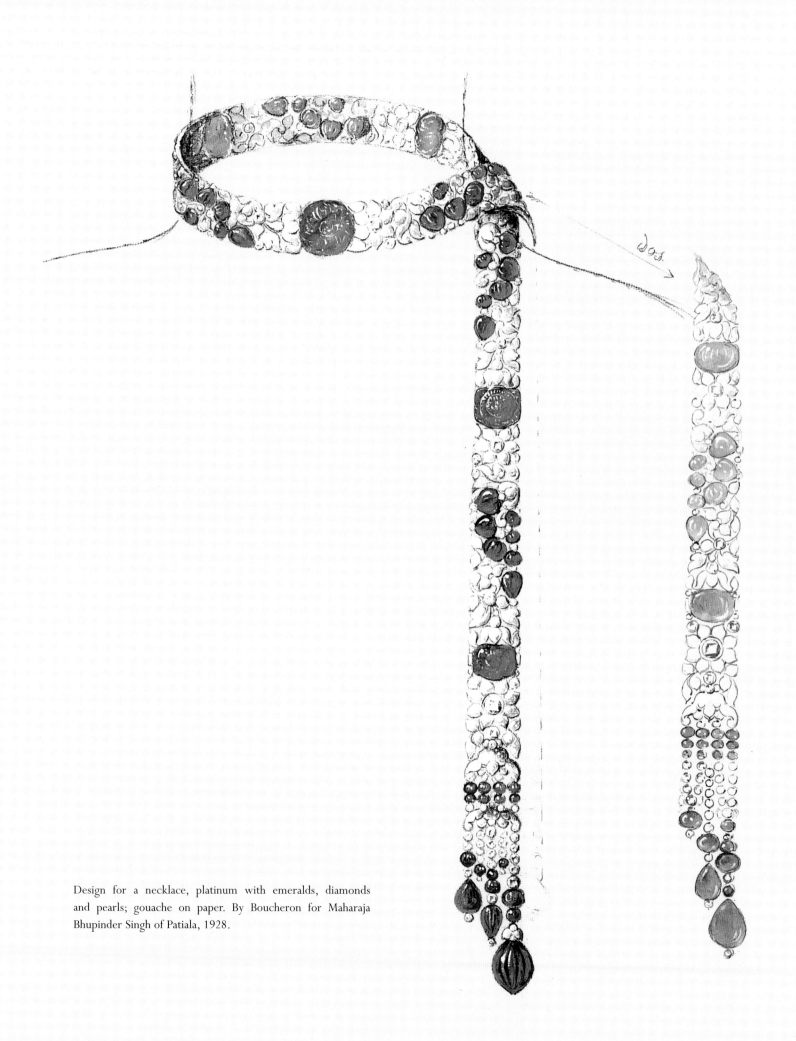

Design for a necklace, platinum with emeralds, diamonds
and pearls; gouache on paper. By Boucheron for Maharaja
Bhupinder Singh of Patiala, 1928.

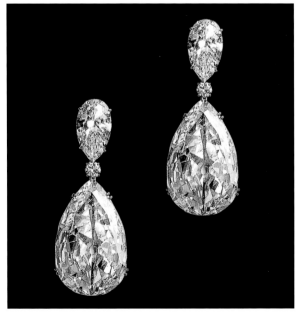

In the early 1910s Maharaja Tukoji Rao Holkar III of Indore purchased from Chaumet two pear-shaped Golconda diamonds of 46.95 and 46.70 carats respectively, thereafter known as the 'Indore Pears'. Chaumet and other leading jewellers proposed various designs for setting the stones, which Maharaja Yeshwant Rao Holkar II ultimately sold to Harry Winston in 1946 along with the 56.50 carat Porter Rhodes diamond.

ABOVE LEFT AND RIGHT: Two designs for a necklace, platinum set with precious stones and diamonds, including the Indore Pears; gouache on paper. By Mauboussin for Maharaja Yeshwant Rao Holkar II of Indore, 1938.

RIGHT: The Indore Pears changed hands repeatedly after 1946. This pair of earrings shows them after Harry Winston had the stones recut to 44.62 and 44.18 carats respectively.

Design for a shoulder ornament, platinum set with diamonds and emeralds, including the Indore Pears; watercolour and gouache on paper. By Joseph Chaumet for Maharaja Tukoji Rao Holkar III of Indore, c. 1911.

DRESS AND ACCESSORIES

∾◡∽

'...IT IS ONLY PROPER THAT INDIAN NOBLEMEN, HOWEVER
MUCH THEY MAY LIKE TO WEAR EUROPEAN CLOTHES
ORDINARILY, SHOULD ON ALL STATE FUNCTIONS WEAR
NATIONAL COSTUME, PARTICULARLY THEIR
NATIONAL OR TRIBAL STATE HEAD-DRESS.'

Maharaja Jagatjit Singh of Kapurthala,
My Travels in Europe and America, 1895

FACING PAGE: Maharaja Yeshwant Rao Holkar II of Indore by Man Ray, c. 1930. Man Ray photographed the maharaja and his wife on several occasions, and the three became friends, sharing a passion for jazz music and dancing. At one photo session Man Ray remembered how 'A record was put on and the young couple danced while I played the accompaniment with drumsticks, cymbals and foot-pedal thumping the valise.'

I n a colonial context the choice of dress worn by an Indian situated him both socially and politically. This was particularly true in light of early 19th century East India Company policy, which aimed to demarcate the British as rulers and Indians as the ruled. The distinction between the races was reinforced through a series of regulations that prevented British officials from wearing Indian clothes and stopped Indians below a certain rank from wearing shoes and boots in the presence of Europeans.[1] The importance of shoes as markers of western civilisation is evident from the comments of Harriet, Marchioness of Dufferin and Ava, who noted on receiving Maharani Sunity Devi of Cooch Behar (1863-1932) that she wore 'native dress, but has very smart shoes and stockings, while here sisters and sisters-in-law had bare feet'.[2] One generation later Maharani Indira Devi of Cooch Behar (1892-1968), although comfortable in western clothes, pointedly chose to appear in traditional Indian bare feet when paying homage to Queen Mary at Buckingham Palace as a symbol of her Indian heritage.[3]

Sartorial segregation reflected popular British perceptions about the superiority of all things European, including garments.[4] This was matched by a belief that the highly structured dress of the British reflected their moral rectitude and the loose, free-formed clothes worn by Indians represented the moral laxity of the subjugated peoples.[5] For some Indians, wearing the 'clothes of the Ruling Race' symbolised both modernity and pro-British ideology.[6] The artist Emily Merrick (b. 1842) encountered a concrete example of this attitude in the widow of Vijayarama Gajapathi Raju, Maharaja of Vizianagram (r. 1845-79):

> I thought the old Maharanee was rather curiously dressed for an Indian lady, but she told me that when she was painted she wished to look like Queen Victoria, and had therefore dressed herself in English costume. She was wearing a purple pork-pie hat trimmed with three diamond stars, and a white veil covered with gold spangles hanging down the back; a purple velvet dress with a broad lace collar fastened by a large broach, and open sleeves lined with white satin and edged with a *ruche*. As the velvet dress was made quite tight, and it was ninety-five in the shade, she must have been extremely uncomfortable. She asked me if I did not think the dress very handsome, and, not liking to disappoint her, I said it was.[7]

The maharani was not the only Indian princess to imitate the dress of Queen Victoria (r. 1837-1901). An official portrait of Sunity Devi of Cooch Behar, taken in London by Lafayette, at the time of the coronation of Edward VII (r. 1901-10), reveals an even closer parallel with images of the ruler, both in posture and attitude (p. 39).

The dress worn by Sunity Devi had been made for her by a French milliner, although her usual London dressmaker was Madame Oliver Holmes.[8] European tailors and couturiers were naturally much in demand among westernised Indian princes, who ordered clothes and uniforms while they were in Europe and supplemented their wardrobes by mail order once they returned home. Firms such as Henry Poole & Co. catered to an international clientele and kept rubbings of clothes and details of measurements from which they were able to cut new garments for commissions from around the world (p. 109). The shoemakers John Lobb & Co. likewise retained foot measurements for the same purpose (pp. 122-3). The accounts of Maharaja Ganga Singh of Bikaner (r. 1887-1943) and his successor, Maharaja Sadul Singh (r. 1943-50), are replete with references to the purchase of clothes and shoes from London firms. A list of 'things to be ordered immediately in England' include khaki socks, silk ties, starched collars, silk handkerchiefs, a motoring cap, an opera hat, flannel trousers, suiting fabric, suits, complete morning dress, 'Nice Tennis or Polo Sweater' and accessories for uniforms.[9] Transactions were rarely simple, with details verified back and forth between Bikaner and London. For instance, Peal & Co.'s invoice of August 1948 for shoes, which listed no fewer than twenty-two items ordered by Sadul Singh, met with protracted correspondence from the Master of the Household about the exact material used for the soles of certain of his shoes (p. 120).[10]

Whether or not in purdah, from the late 19th century onwards Indian princesses began wearing western garments and ordering their trousseaus in Europe. Begum Kaikhusrau Jahan of Bhopal (r. 1901-26), for instance, often wore European clothes under her *burkha*.[11] The daughters of Maharaja Nripendra Narayan of Cooch Behar (r. 1863-1911) were completely comfortable in Indian and western dress, having 'danced through the ball-rooms of London and Calcutta in the smartest Parisian toilettes, and were as much at home in the Park or at a gala night at the Opera as in their own country'.[12] Indian princesses also commissioned the leading designers of the day. Among them was Indira Devi of Cooch Behar. In his autobiography, Salvatore Ferragamo (1898-1960) recalled her order for more than one hundred pairs of shoes, among them a pair made with pearls and diamonds supplied by the princess herself: 'I made one pair of shoes in green velvet with a spiral of pearls running up the heals and one in black velvet with a diamond buckle and two straight rows of diamonds running down the heel.'[13] For another, unnamed Indian princess, Ferragamo used the feathers of a hummingbird to create the rarest and most highly priced shoes of his career.[14] Rani Sita Devi of Kapurthala (1915-2002), considered one of the best dressed women in the world, and Australian-born Rani Molly of Pudukkottai (1894-1967) ordered clothes from the latest French designers, among them Callot Soeurs, Jeanne Paquin, Jean Patou, Madeleine Vionnet and Elsa Schiaparelli, Edward Molyneux, Coco Channel and Jeanne Lanvin (pp. 110-13). It wasn't only western-style clothes that were custom-made in Europe for Indian royals. Monsieur Erigua of Paris produced fashionable chiffons in sari lengths for Indira Devi of Cooch Behar, and Parisian firms such as Sarees Inc. specialised in creating for elite Indian women rare sari materials in the latest western fabrics and patterns (p. 115).[15]

With western education, wearing European clothes became increasingly common among Indian princes, although traditional headdress was sometimes retained. When Man Ray (1890-1976) photographed Aga Khan III (1877-1957), he expected to find 'a vision of Oriental splendour with silks and turbans, pearls, emeralds and rubies'. Instead the prince appeared 'wearing a yellow woollen sweater, doeskin trousers and – a pair of boxing gloves on his hands. He explained that since he spent so much of his time in Europe and England, his subjects would be most impressed to see him in a western outfit.'[16] Man Ray likewise observed that during his photo session with Maharaja Yeshwant Rao Holkar II of Indore (r. 1926-61), the prince wore only 'western clothes–sack suits and formal evening dress'.[17] The photographer portrayed Maharani Sanyogita of Indore (1914-37) in a sari and in western dress. On one occasion she posed in 'French clothes, and a huge emerald ring. The maharaja had bought it for her that morning while taking a walk.'[18] Not every prince was convinced that adopting western clothes was the best way forward. Venkata Sweta Chalapati Ranga Rao, ruler of Bobbili (r. 1887-1926), for instance, produced a volume aimed at the 'Indian Aristocracy', in which he stressed the importance for Indians of maintaining their cultural integrity, including their own style of clothes. Western dress, he wrote, was not unattractive, 'but it is purely European, and so unfitted for Hindus'.[19] For others it was comfort, rather than any point of principle, that mediated against wearing western clothes. Meherban Narayanrao Babashaeb, Chief of Ichalkaranji, found simply that it was 'difficult to understand the utility of stiff collars and tight-fitting boots and shoes. Whatever may be the reason for them (and they serve a really

useful purpose no doubt), there is no denying their discomfort, which Europeans themselves admit. I know of nothing more calculated to upset one's equanimity than the struggle involved in the adjustment of a new and highly-glazed English collar, unless it be the ordeal of becoming accustomed to the torture of narrow boots.'[20] In his diary, the Rajput nobleman Amar Singh (1879-1942) concurred. When in 1904 he joined the Indian Army, he was ordered to wear western clothes and found it 'an awful lot of trouble to wear new collars and neckties which I have begun using from today.'[21]

European-style clothes were embellished with appropriate western accessories. For instance, Mir Mahboob Ali Khan, Nizam of Hyderabad (r. 1869-1911), who commissioned a 240-foot long wardrobe for his clothes, ordered cufflinks, watch chains and a pocket watch to wear when dressed in a suit.[22] Raja Rajaram of Kolhapur (r. 1866-70) also purchased a watch on his trip to Europe, and on his venture to India in 1911, Jacques Cartier (1885-1942) found that maharajas wanted 'pocket-watches', at that time 'high fashion in Paris and London.'[23] The young jeweller sold Maharaja Jagatjit Singh of Kapurthala (r. 1877-1949) an example in blue enamel, Nizam Osman Ali Khan of Hyderabad (r. 1911-67) an example in gold, Jam Saheb Ranjitsinhji of Nawanagar (r. 1907-33) a pocket watch in platinum and Aga Khan III one ornamented with pavé diamonds. Such was the demand for pocket-watches among princes that London firm J.W. Benson advertised an 'Imperial Watch' specially aimed at the maharaja market. The covers of these could be personalised with a prince's portrait and his coat of arms in enamel (p. 130). Such personalised watches carried on into the modern age. Jaeger-LeCoultre's Reverso watch was ideally-suited for polo-playing princes, who needed only to flip the case to ensure the safety of their watch in the event of a match. For Maharaja Man Singh II of Jaipur (r. 1922-1970) the firm created a reverso with the emblem of the Sawaiman Guards on the reverse, for distribution to the ruler's favourite officers (p. 134). Cufflinks and tie-pins, cigarette cases and lighters, jewelled handbags, belt-buckles, lipstick holders and cosmetic cases all appear among the accessories purchased by Indian royalty from western houses. Goods from stock were supplemented with commissions from leading luxury houses. Among the most fantastic of these were the two gold tongue-scrapers designed for Sita Devi of Baroda (1917-86) by Van Cleef & Arpels (pp. 137-38).

Maharaja Bhupinder Singh of Patiala by Vandyk, 1931. The maharaja was fond of decorations, as is evident from the profusion of medals on his chest. In addition to those awarded him, he purchased badges and medals from Spink and Son. The Medal Gallery in the Sheesh Mahal, Patiala, is the largest of its kind and includes not only foreign medals but also those created by the maharaja as recognition for services offered by his own people.

LEGION OF HONOUR · DECORATION du JUILLET 1830 · BLACK STAR OF BENIN · ORDER OF CAMBODIA · ORDER OF THE DRAGON ANNAM · STAR OF D'ANJOUN · MEDAILLE MILITAIRE

THE ORDER OF CHRIST PORTUGAL · THE ORDER OF VICTOSA PORTUGAL · ORDER OF NICHAN IFTIKHAR TUNIS · THE ORDER OF OSMANIEH TURKEY

THE ORDER OF THE LION AND SUN PERSIA

THE MADONNA · THE ORDER OF RANJIT SINGH · THE ORDER OF LEOPOLD BELGIUM · STAR OF ETHIOPIA ABYSSINIA · THE ORDER OF DANILO MONTENEGRO

THE LEVANT FRANCE · MEDAL FOR 1870-71 FRANCE · PRESENTED BY PRESIDENT POINCARE MAY 1917 · CRIMEA · FRENCH ITALIAN 1859 · EXPEDITION TO CHINA 1860 FRANCE · TOKIN, CHINA, ANNAM 1883-1885 · MEDAL du JUILLET 1830 · MEDAL MONTEN

GARRARD & Co L^{TD}
CROWN JEWELLERS.

TELEGRAMS,"EMPEARL,PICCY, LONDON."
TELEPHONE, REGENT 0757 (3 LINES)

Established in the
HAYMARKET 1721.

24, ALBEMARLE STREET,
LONDON, W.I.

ACM/EB.

28th May 1946.

The Private Secretary,
  to His Highness The Maharaja of Bikaner,
    Bikaner House,
      Abu,
        (Rajputana - India)

Sir,

      We beg to thank you for your letter of the 11th May 1946 your reference 116. PS/C concerning the "Vikram Badge." received together with enclosures as stated.

      The details and instructions regarding the Badge in its various Classes and sizes are quite clear and we will proceed to consider the cost of making the necessary dies and tools and the cost of producing the Badge from them.

      We will write to you on this subject as soon as we are ready.

      There are two points of which you make no mention and they are the colour and width of the ribbon and the colour of the cases to contain the Insignia. Perhaps you will let us know your decision in these matters at your convenience.

        Yours faithfully,

        Garrard & Co. ld.

Letter from Garrard & Co. about a commission from Maharaja Sadul Singh of Bikaner for making the Vikram Badge, 1946. From the late 19th century onwards it became standard practice for Indian states to create orders and decorations along western models. The Vikram Badge was instituted as recognition for services rendered to the ruler and royal family of Bikaner. The badge and star had an image of Rao Bika, the founder of the state, and a Devanagari inscription which translated to: 'Blessing by Karni Mata for her perpetual rule.'

FACING PAGE: Thakur Hari Singh by Lafayette, 1896. This photograph was taken when the sitter visited London in the service of Sir Pratap Singh, who was attending the celebrations for Queen Victoria's Diamond Jubilee. The thakur wears the full dress uniform of the Jodhpur Imperial Service Lancers. The costume fuses the traditional turban, kurta and *patka* (sash) with elements taken from western military wear such as the epaulettes, braids, cord, belt and boots.

633   The Maharaja Gaekwar of Baroda G.C.S.I.

Messrs. Henry Poole and Co. London.

You are hereby appointed

Tailors

To His Highness
The Maharaja Gaekwar of Baroda

Given under my hand

at Hyde Park Hotel, London.

this 26th day of July 1905.

Sayajirao Gaekwar

105

FACING PAGE: Ledger for Gaekwar Sayajirao III of Baroda from the account books of Henry Poole & Co., 1903-10.
INSET: Gaekwar Sayajirao III of Baroda by Bassano, 1934.
As the accounts of Henry Poole & Co. demonstrate, Indian princes were regular clients of Savile Row tailors.

Warrant from Gaekwar Sayajirao III of Baroda to Henry Poole and Co., 1905. Sayajirao followed the European royal convention of awarding a Warrant of Appointment to distinguished tradesmen who served the royal household. This warrant recognises the ruler's patronage of the distinguished Savile Row firm Henry Poole & Co.

Design for a ceremonial sword mounted with rubies and diamonds; watercolour and gouache on paper. By Joseph Chaumet, c. 1910.

FACING PAGE: Design for a ceremonial coat, cloth, worked with precious stones; watercolour and gouache on paper. By Joseph Chaumet, c. 1910.

It is likely that Chaumet produced these designs not for a particular prince, but simply to appeal to potential Indian clients.

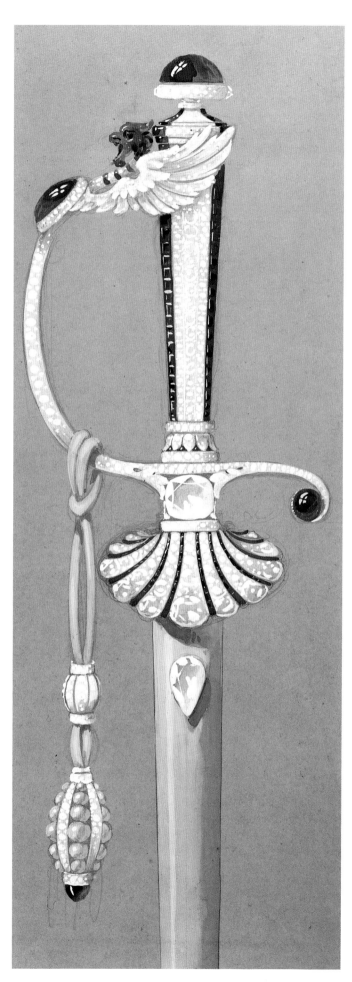

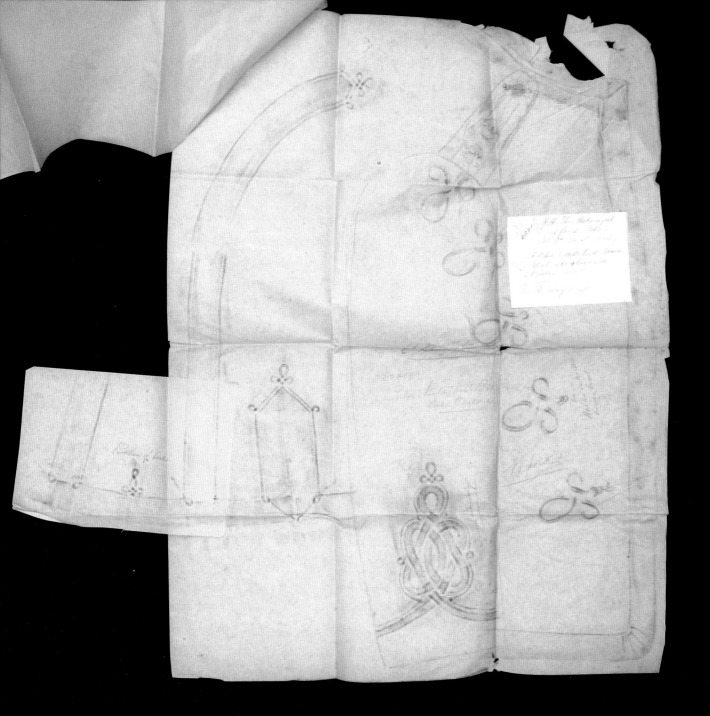

Rubbing of a coat, pencil on tracing paper. Made by Henry Poole & Co., for
Maharaja Nripendra Narayan of Cooch Behar, c. 1899.

FACING PAGE: Maharaja Nripendra Narayan of Cooch Behar by Lafayette, 1899.
The ruler is shown wearing the dismounted order review uniform of a British
Officer of the 6th Bengal Cavalry. Among his decorations are the Star, Sash and
Badge of a Grand Commander of the Order of the Indian Empire. The uniform
was almost certainly made for him by Henry Poole & Co., whose archives
retain the original paper rubbings of uniforms designed for the prince.

Rani Molly of Pudukkottai, by Vandyk, c. 1920. Melbourne-born Esmé Mary Fink met Raja Martanda of Pudukkottai in Sydney while he was touring Australia. The couple married in 1915, but Rani Molly was denied the title Her Highness and was initially not received in official circles. Their son Martanda Sydney was excluded from the succession on the grounds of his mixed blood. Ultimately the raja appointed his brother regent and settled in Cannes, where the couple moved in fashionable circles. Molly was a regular client of Callot Soeurs, Jean Paquin, Jean Patou, Madeleine Vionnet, Elsa Schiaparelli, Edward Molyneux and Jeanne Lanvin.

FACING PAGE: Dress, silk, embroidered with pearls. By Jean Paquin, 1928 for Rani Molly of Pudukkottai.

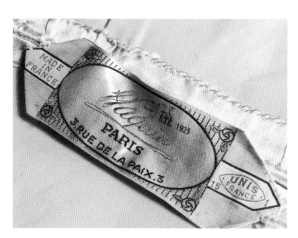

113

FACING PAGE LEFT: House coat, silk, embroidered. By Capdeville for Rani Molly of Pudukkottai, 1930.

FACING PAGE RIGHT: Evening coat, silk brocade with silk velvet. By Jean Paquin for Rani Molly of Pudukkottai, 1922. LEFT: Evening dress, machine-made lace. By Callot Soeurs for Rani Molly of Pudukkottai, 1937.

ABOVE: Labels from Paquin from a silk dress, 1928 (previous page) and an evening coat, 1922 (facing page).

114

LEFT: Rani Sita Devi of Kapurthala, c. 1940. The royal house of Kapurthala developed strong links with France, eventually acquiring a residence in Paris. In this photograph the rani poses against an image of the Eiffel Tower.

RIGHT: Rani Sita Devi of Kapurthala, c. 1940. The princess poses in French chiffon, the choicest sari material of the period.

SAREES (FRANCE) LTD

Société à Responsabilité limitée - Capital 1.500.000 frs - R.C. Seine 148.455

Manufacturers of silk Chiffon Sarees
plain, printed, embroidered, painted
Hundred shades and patterns
exclusive designs

TRADE MARK "FRANCEIFFEL"

TELEPHONE : OPÉ. 36·37
RIC. 75·41

CABLE ADDRESS :
STEDIAMA·PARIS

15, BOULEVARD DE LA MADELEINE

PARIS (I)   27th August 1957.

The Secretary to
Her Highness Maharani Shantadevi
Gaekwar of Baroda
Laxmi Vilas Palace,
Baroda
Inde

Dear Sir,

        We have the pleasure to acknowledge receipt of your letter
10th August and according to your instructions we have posted to Her
Highness the Maharani a very comprehensive range of samples of several qualities plain and printed Pure Silk French Chiffon.

        May we respectfully ask Her Highness to make several selec-
tions should some of the selected patterns or colours be out of
stock; we need not emphasize on the fact that these swatches of
samples are extremely costly and not only do we rely on receiving
a large order but after selection will Her Highness kindly hand
over the samples to some of Her relations of friends so that they
may send us their orders and it is our intention to ask them in
turn to proceed in the same way so that our samples may serve the
purpose of many buyers. In this way we can keep our prices as low
as possible and we shall say that we have not put up our prices at
all for the past four years which is an extraordinary feat as every
one all over the world are increasing their prices.

        Lastly we shall point out that due to export devaluation
you can send your remittance in francs from India or England at the
rate of 1160 Fr per £ which is showing a very substantial rebate on
previous prices.

        We have also the pleasure to inform you that we can accept
payment in Rupes in the form of 100 Rupes notes at 80 Francs per
rupe and in this way the Laparisian Sarees will cost only Rs 30/-
each which is lower than before.

        Let us hope Her Highness the Maharani will appreciate
our offer and with our respectful and devoted regards to Their
Highness the Maharaja and the Maharani,

Received 30-8-57
URL.

                                        Yours sincerely,
                                        SAREES (France) Ltd
                                        Le Gerant,

T/MP

Letter from Sarees Ltd. to Maharani Shantidevi of Baroda, 1957. The
correspondence reveals the prevailing taste among royal women for
saris of imported French silk chiffon.

Rani Sita Devi of Kapurthala, c. 1935. In her day the princess was considered one of the best dressed women in the world. In this photograph she wears the dramatic Tangerine Velvet headdress by the renowned firm of Reboux and a silver fox coat designed by Mainbocher, the American couturier who created the wedding dress worn by Wallis Simpson at her 1937 marriage to the Duke of Windsor.

FACING PAGE: Rani Sita Devi of Kapurthala, by Cecil Beaton, c. 1940. The rani was a daughter of Raja Udai Raj Singh of Kashipur and was married to Karamjit Singh, younger son of Maharaja Jagatjit Singh of Kapurthala. Her intelligence–she was fluent in English, French and German–was matched by an innate sense of style. In this photograph Beaton evokes fashion photography of Man Ray.

118

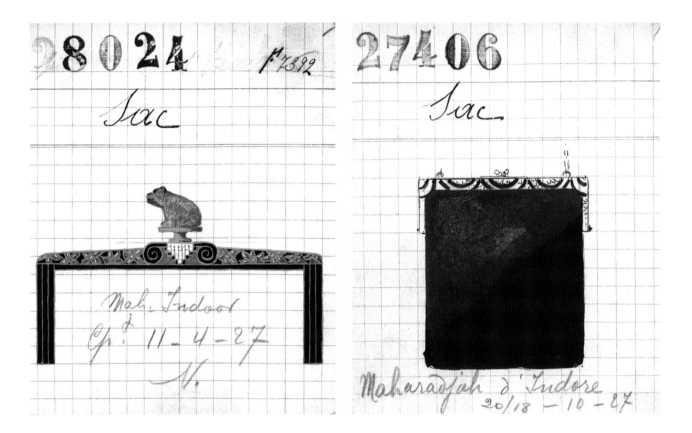

LEFT: Design for a purse, gold with enamel; gouache on card. Made by Van Cleef & Arpels, 1926 and purchased by Maharaja Tukoji Rao Holkar III of Indore, 1927.

RIGHT: Design for a purse, silk and platinum set with diamonds and onyx; gouache on card. Made by Van Cleef & Arpels and purchased by Maharaja Tukoji Rao Holkar III Indore, 1927.

LEFT: Design for a powder compact, gold and platinum set with rubies and diamonds; gouache on card. Made by Van Cleef & Arpels, 1937 and purchased by Maharani Sita Devi of Baroda, 1959. The floral clips could be removed and worn as jewellery.

RIGHT: Design for a necessaire, gold with black and red enamel, diamonds and silk; gouache and ink on card. Made by Van Cleef & Arpels, 1925, and purchased by Maharani Sita Devi of Baroda, 1946.

GOVERNMENT OF BIKANER.

Notes and Orders.

M.H.

I send herewith a statement showing the various particulars of boots, shoes &c., required to be given to the firm when ordering them. H.H. has ordered that future orders should be made on such a form to obviate any misunderstanding and help to get the order correctly executed.

2.   This might be noted in the Standing Orders.

Private Secretary.

Bikaner,
M/27.2.49.

PEAL & CO

F. C. PEAL.   G. L. PEAL.   C. F. PEAL.
J. R. PEAL.   R. O. PEAL.
FOUNDED 1791

Incorporating

FLACK & SMITH
Boot Makers

**487, OXFORD STREET
LONDON. W.I.**
NEAR MARBLE ARCH

CABLEGRAMS – PEALBOOTS, LONDON.

BOOT MAKERS
BY APPOINTMENT
TO THE LATE KING GEORGE V.

BOOT MAKERS
BY APPOINTMENT
TO THE PRINCE OF WALES
1920-1936

NEW YORK ADDRESS.
THE BILTMORE
MADISON AVENUE AT 43RD STREET.
NEW YORK CITY.
TELEPHONE NO. MURRAY HILL 9-7920.

K
WAC/MR.

August 5th, 1948.

His Highness, The Maharaja, of Bikaner.

List of Orders in hand

1 pair of black Riding boots, short lacing in neck	£23	7	6
1 set Long Hollow trees	6	17	6
1 pair single strap spurs, fitted with spur pads & leathers, 1 pair boot garters	3	4	0
1 pair drab cloth slippers, black binding	2	7	0
1 pair black brogued shoes SMART TOE	11	0	0
1 pair trees	1	12	6
1 pair dark reverse calf Veldt Schoens (suede finish) ROUND TOE leather soles with corrugated rubber on top	11	12	6
1 pair trees	1	12	6
1 pair black leather Friar shoes "Spoon" on fronts Jeddite rubber soles ROUND TOE	11	0	0
1 pair trees	1	12	6
1 pair patent leather pumps with bows SMART TOE	6	17	6
1 pair trees	1	12	6
1 pair brown Tank boots ROUND TOE	14	15	0
1 pair trees	2	12	6
1 pair brown leather shoes (open fronts) leather soles with corrugated rubber on top ROUND TOE	11	0	0
1 pair trees	1	12	6
1 pair dark brown reverse calf (suede finish) and brown leather brogued shoes Jeddite rubber soles ROUND TOE	11	10	0
1 pair trees	1	12	6
1 pair white and black brogued Monk shoes	11	15	0
1 pair trees	1	12	6
1 pair patent leather evening shoes SMART TOE	10	2	6
1 pair trees	1	12	6

Copy of letter No.WAC/JEH D/-4-10-48 from M/s Peal & Co., 487, Oxford Street, London W.I. ENG. to Lt.-Col. Kishan Singh, Master of the Household, to H.H. The Maharaja of Bikaner, Hotel Plaza-Athenee, Paris, France.

--

Further to your letter of 12th August, 1948, in the second paragraph, you mention that the Tank boots should be made with single waterproof soles, as on the walking boots previously supplied to His Highness. We note, however, that on the statement which you sent us detailing the orders, Jeddite rubber soles are ordered.

We have entered the order to have stout single substance leather soles, with small nails round the edge, and rubber heels. This conforms with the instructions in your letter. The remaining items have been checked, and amended where necessary.

Assuring you of our best attention at all times.

S/-
15-10-48.

RR No. 902/PS
15/10/48

An 3993 Df 15-X-48.
Copy forwarded for information and favour of necessary action.

15-10-48.

FACING PAGE: Documents relating to an order for shoes from Peal & Co., by Maharaja Sadul Singh of Bikaner, 1948-49. Indian rulers regularly ordered western clothes and accessories from favoured firms in Europe. These letters between Bikaner and the London shoemakers provide an idea of the voluminous correspondence required in obtaining custom-ordered shoes at long distance.

Slippers, velvet with embroidery of metal thread. Made by Hellstern & Sons, for Maharaja Jagatjit Singh of Kapurthala, c. 1920. These slippers are in an Indian style but were made in France by a firm of celebrated shoemakers which was based in Place Vendome. The company specialised in luxury footware, and particularly worked with rich materials and beading.

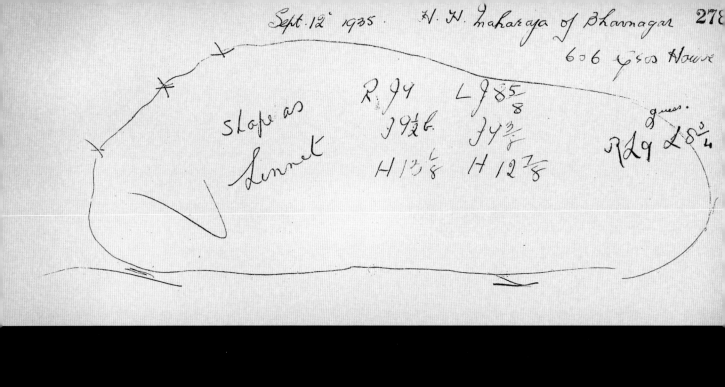

ABOVE: Foot outline of Maharaja Krishnakumarsinhji Bhavsinhji of Bhavnagar, pencil on paper. By John Lobb, 1935.

BELOW: Foot outline of Nawab Iftikhar Ali Khan of Pataudi, pencil on paper. By John Lobb, c. 1930.

FACING PAGE ABOVE: Foot outline of Maharaja Man Singh II of Jaipur, pencil on paper. By John Lobb, c. 1930.

FACING PAGE BELOW: Shoes, leather. Made by John Lobb, for Maharaja Paramjit Singh of Kapurthala, c. 1950.

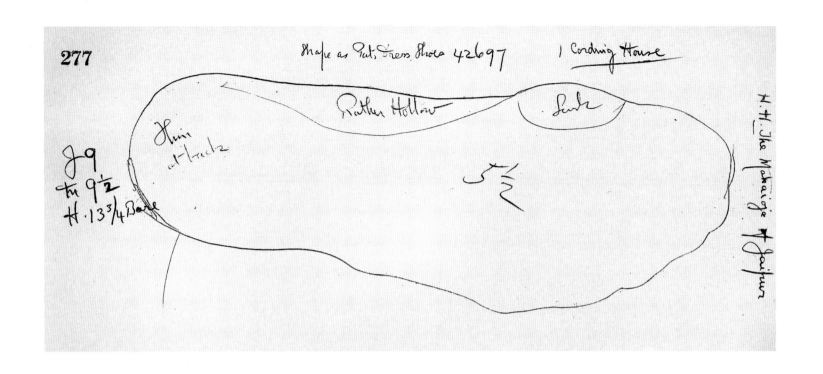

The London shoemakers John Lobb recorded foot outlines of foreign clients in readiness for future orders received from abroad.

Sandal, leather with multicoloured beads. Made by Ferragamo for Maharani Indira Devi of Cooch Behar, 1938. In his memoirs Salvatore Ferragamo recalled extraordinary commissions from the maharani, among them a pair of shoes in green velvet encrusted with pearls and a pair in black velvet set with diamonds.

FACING PAGE: Maharani Indira Devi of Cooch Behar, 1934. This photograph captures something of the legendary beauty of the maharani, who was a leading client of European designers of the day. The princess is wearing a chiffon sari which was almost certainly acquired through retailers who specialised in selling Indian garments made from luxurious French textiles.

Indira Devi
1934

127

TOP: Belt buckle, platinum set with diamonds and onyx. Made by Cartier for Maharani Sanyogita of Indore, 1928.

BOTTOM: Belt buck, platinum, gold and black enamel, set with diamonds. Made by Cartier for Maharaja Bhupinder Singh of Patiala, 1930.

Repeater pocket watch, gold, with a photographic portrait of Maharaja Sardar Singh of Jodhpur, c. 1900. The watch is mounted with a miniature photograph of the young ruler.

FACING PAGE: Repeater pocket watch, gold and enamel, with a portrait of Maharaja Jaswant Singh II of Jodhpur, c. 1880. The exterior of the case is decorated with the ruler's arms and equestrian subjects, including polo, show jumping and racing. Inscriptions feature the ruler's name in Persian and Devanagri script on one side of the case, and in English on the other.

130

Advertisement for 'The Imperial Watch' from the firm of J.W. Benson Ltd, from an undated catalogue, c. 1880. This London firm produced personalised pocket watches for Indian princes, with their portrait on one side, and their arms on the other. Such business was conducted by mail order as is suggested by the text: a 'photograph and sketch of the Arms required to be mounted on the watch should be sent with order.' The watch advertised was made for Maharaja Tukoji Rao Holkar II of Indore for £1,085. The portrait is taken from a photograph by Bourne and Shepherd in 1877.

FACING PAGE: Repeater pocket watch, gold with enamel portrait of Maharaja Bhupinder Singh of Patiala, c. 1920. One side of the watch case is decorated with the ruler's image, the other with his arms.

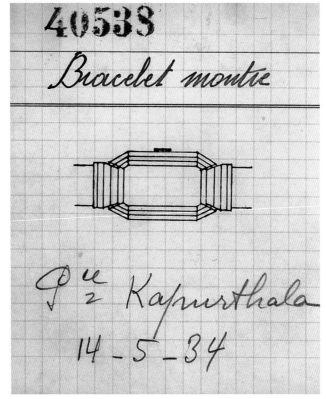

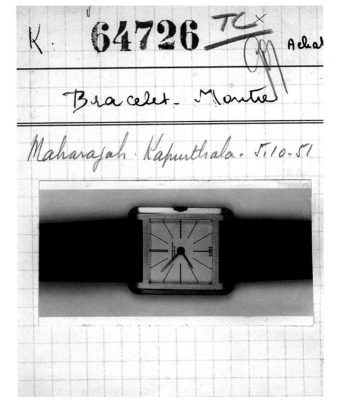

132

TOP: Design for a watch, ink on card. Made by Van Cleef & Arpels and purchased by Paramjit Singh of Kapurthala, 1935.

BOTTOM: Design for a watch, ink on card. Made by Van Cleef & Arpels and purchased by Maharaja Jagatjit Singh of Kapurthala, 1933.

TOP: Design for a wristwatch, ink on card. Made by Van Cleef & Arpels and purchased by Paramjit Singh of Kapurthala, 1934.

BOTTOM: Wristwatch, white gold. Made by Van Cleef & Arpels and purchased by Maharaja Paramjit Singh of Kapurthala, 1951. The movement was the work of the Swiss firm, Audemars-Piguet.

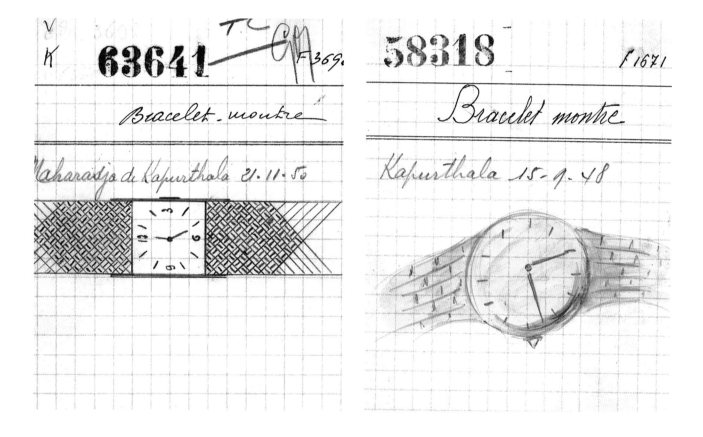

Design for a wristwatch with gold bracelet; ink on card. Made by Van Cleef & Arpels and purchased by Maharaja Paramjit Singh of Kapurthala, 1950.

Design for a wristwatch with gold bracelet; gouache and pencil on card. Made by Van Cleef & Arpels, 1947 and purchased by Maharaja Jagatjit Singh of Kapurthala, 1948.

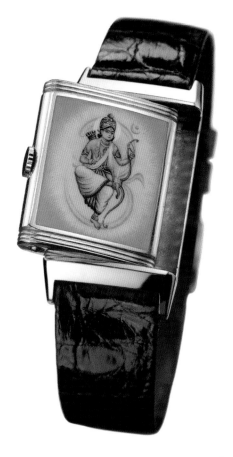

RIGHT AND ABOVE LEFT: Wristwatch, 'Reverso Sawaiman Guards', steel with enamel. Made by Jaeger-LeCoultre, for Maharaja Man Singh II of Jaipur, c. 1935. The idea of a reversible watch face was developed by Jaeger-LeCoultre around 1930 for polo-players in India. This example was made as one of a special order destined for members of Jaipur's elite Sawaiman Guards. The sunburst refers to the Jaipur royal family's *suryavanshi* lineage, through which they claim descent from the sun.

ABOVE CENTRE: Wristwatch, 'Reverso Krishna', steel and gold with enamel. Made by Jaeger-LeCoultre, 1937.

ABOVE RIGHT: Wristwatch, 'Reverso Maharani', gold with enamel. Made by Jaeger-LeCoultre, 1937.

Travel watch, gold with enamel, with applied platinum and diamond monogram. Made by Cartier and purchased by Maharaja Bhupinder Singh of Patiala, 1929.

Wristwatch, 'Tank à guichets', gold with enamel and diamonds. Made by Cartier and purchased by Maharaja Bhupinder Singh of Patiala, 1928.

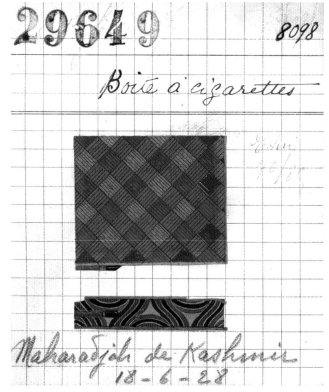

TOP: Design for a cigarette case, gold with enamel; gouache on card. Made by Van Cleef & Arpels and purchased by Maharaja Hari Singh of Jammu and Kashmir, 1928.

BOTTOM: Design for a cigarette case, red gold, with enamel; gouache on card. Made by Van Cleef & Arpels and purchased by Maharaja Hari Singh of Jammu and Kashmir, 1928.

TOP: Design for a cigarette case, gold, woven in three colours, with enamel; gouache on card. Made by Van Cleef & Arpels and purchased by Maharaja Hari Singh of Jammu and Kashmir, 1928.

BOTTOM: Design for a cigarette case, gold and platinum, set with diamonds; gouache and pencil on card. Made by Van Cleef & Arpels and purchased by Maharaja Hari Singh of Jammu and Kashmir, 1928.

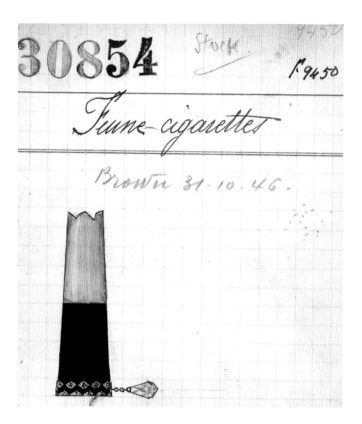

137

TOP: Design for a cigarette holder, platinum, mounted with amber, lapis lazuli, diamonds and a sapphire; gouache and pencil on card. Made by Van Cleef & Arpels, 1928 and purchased by Maharani Sita Devi of Baroda, 1946.

BOTTOM: Design for a cigarette holder, gold and imitation tortoiseshell; gouache and pencil on card. Made by Van Cleef & Arpels, 1946 and acquired by Maharani Sita Devi of Baroda, 1948.

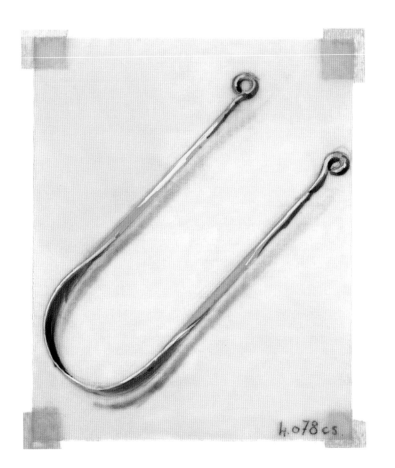

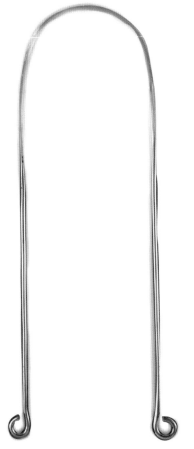

LEFT AND CENTRE: Design for a tongue scraper, gouache and pencil on paper; and corresponding tongue scraper, gold. Made by Van Cleef & Arpels for Maharani Sita Devi of Baroda, 1955. This is one of a pair of tongue scrapers ordered by the client. The commissioning bill indicates that the order was 'trés urgent'.

RIGHT: Design for a comb and comb-case, gold; gouache and pencil on paper. Made by Van Cleef & Arpels for Maharani Sita Devi of Baroda, 1950. This order was accompanied by six replaceable plastic combs that slid into the gold spine.

FACING PAGE: Dressing set, silver, enamel, mirror and coral. Made by Cartier, 1925 and purchased by Maharaja Bhupinder Singh of Patiala. This gentleman's dressing set consists of a total of fifteen pieces executed in a high Art Deco style. Each component is applied with Maharaja Bhupinder Singh's monogram: MBS.

ROYAL LIVING

༄

'THE ARRANGEMENTS OF THE TABLE ARE PERFECT. THE LINEN IS
SPECIALLY WOVEN IN BELFAST; THE PLATES AND DISHES ARE
USUALLY OF SILVER, WITH GOLD FOR GREAT OCCASIONS, AND
THERE SEEMS TO BE AN ENDLESS SUPPLY OF THEM.'

Rev. Edward St Clair Weeden, *A Year with the Gaekwar of Baroda*, 1912.

FACING PAGE: Ice sculptures made for Maharaja Bhupinder Singh of Patiala by the Savoy Hotel, London, during
his stay there in 1921. In honour of the exotic guest the figures are modelled after a camel and elephant.

P rinces living in a western style naturally turned to Europe for the domestic goods they required, importing everything from bed-linen to bathroom fittings. They decorated their palaces with outstanding examples of western design, purchasing splendid and spectacular works from leading craftsmen and designers, and commissioning works that were extravagant, if sometimes curious. In their mission to promote British trade and manufacture, the Government encouraged maharajas to consume luxury goods from British firms, and helped them to cultivate 'a taste for the elegant superfluities of European living'.[1] In a colonial environment enormous kudos was attached to goods imported from the West, which were considered innately superior: 'anything "English" or "imported" at once acquires a special value, and an imported dog, iron bedstead, carpet and article of furniture stamps the owner as a man of taste and means, and sheds dignity over him.'[2]

The concept of the relative purity of materials in Hinduism meant that historically princes ate from metal dishes, usually of gold or silver. Earthenware vessels were considered less pure, and once used were typically thrown away. Muslim rulers, on the other hand, used both metal and a range of ceramics, foremost of which was Chinese porcelain, for which there developed a particular appreciation.[3] With the presence of European trading companies in India, Muslim princes began to commission dinner services from Western porcelain factories. When Lord Valentia (1770-1844) dined at the nawabi court in Lucknow in the early 19th century, he found that the 'service was English, with a profusion of fine cut-glass basons'.[4] Flight Barr and Barr produced a service in the Pompeian style for Nawab Ghazi-ud-din Haidar (r. 1814-27) which was embellished with his monogram, 'NGH' flanked by the twin fish of Lucknow and a pair of standing tigers, surmounted by a *katar* (punch dagger; p. 145).[5] Archival material at the Spode Museum indicates that when, in 1819, the nawab was elevated to the rank of king, he commissioned an exceptionally fine service decorated with similar motifs, but surmounted by a western-style crown, an indication of his new rank.[6] Through the Madras-based agents Griffiths, Cooke & Co., Azam Jah, Nawab of Arcot (r. 1819-25) ordered an equally magnificent dinner service of more than one thousand pieces made by Chamberlain's Worcester (p. 144).[7]

With the construction of western-style palaces after the establishment of the Raj, it became matter of course for all princes to order monogrammed or armorial dinner services from Europe.

Among the most significant services of this later period are two painted sets of plates produced by Royal Worcester for Ranjitsinhji, Jam Saheb of Nawanagar (r. 1907-33).[8] Their decoration speaks volumes about the dual-identity of the prince. The plates intended to be used in the ruler's house outside London, in Staines, depicted scenes in and around Nawanagar, while the plates dispatched to India were painted with the English scenes that he most loved (pp. 160-61). Gaekwar Sayajirao III of Baroda (r. 1875-1939) commissioned Royal Worcester to produce an exceptional set of hand-painted plates decorated with scenes from Hindu mythology (pp. 158-59) The use of western-style dinner services reflected the trend among princes for serving food in the European style. Many princely states maintained separate kitchens for European food, often under a French or English chef. Maharani Indira of Cooch Behar (1892-1968) was so discerning about her cuisine that she took her Indian cook to Alfredo's in Rome so that he could understand the flavour of his distinctive lasagne![9] While at Le Touquet, the same princess introduced her children to the delights of frogs' legs by pretending to them that the delicious meat was chicken.[10]

Princes regularly purchased silver plate and cutlery from the many European silversmiths who worked in India, among which were the leading firms of Hamilton & Co., Calcutta, and P. Orr & Sons, Madras. Considerable quantities of silver were also imported from London. Garrard's, for example, developed a steady business in India as did the Goldsmiths and Silversmiths Company, whose extravagant shop on Regent Street had a separate entrance for its colonial showroom.[11] Maharaja Bhupinder Singh of Patiala (r. 1900-38) was a leading client, and in time for the visit to his state in 1922 of Edward, Prince of Wales (1894-1972), commissioned a substantial silver-gilt dinner service from the firm at a cost of £30,000, the contemporary equivalent of buying fourteen Rolls-Royces (pp. 166-67).[12] The shape of the various dishes follow western conventions, but many of the pieces are artfully styled with an Indian touch. Perhaps the most unusual work commissioned by an Indian prince from a European silversmith was the silver-encrusted bed which Sadiq Muhammad Khan, Nawab of Bahawalpur (r. 1866-99) ordered from Christofle through the agencies of the firm Aron Brothers (pp. 174-75). Whether the design of this piece was inspired by the prince's own fantasies, or prompted by his agents is difficult to know. The order submitted to Christofle in 1882 called for a bed of 'dark wood decorated with applied sterling with gilded parts, monograms and arms, ornamented with four life-size bronze figures painted in flesh colour with natural hair, movable eyes and arms, holding fans and horse tails.'[13] The production of such a piece required the skills of diverse craftsmen, including a silversmith (290 kilograms of silver were used to decorate the bed), a sculptor, a cabinet-maker, an automaton-maker and a hairdresser. The bed itself was eastern in effect, with a cusped head and foot-board embellished with rich foliate decoration. By contrast, the four naked figures were European, representing women of France, Spain, Italy and Greece, each with varying skin-tone and hair colour. Through ingenious mechanics linked to the mattress, the nawab was able to set the alluring figures in motion so that they fanned him while winking, all against a thirty-minute cycle of music from Gounod's *Faust* generated by a music box crafted by the firm of Thibouville et Lamy. It was perhaps discretion that prevented Sadiq Muhammad Khan from revealing his identity to Christofle; the company only discovered that he was the patron behind this extraordinary order in 1983.

The Bahawalpur Bed represents a broader Indian princely fascination with automata and mechanical toys, evident, for instance, in *Tipu's Tiger*, a painted wooden model of a tiger mauling a European soldier which contains a mechanical organ and bellows capable of generating both the tiger's roar and the soldier's shriek. The mechanism is western, and is thought to have been made by a Frenchman working at the court of Tipu Sultan (r. 1782-99).[14] Western-made automata fascinated later rulers of Mysore as well, as is apparent from the diary of the artist Emily Merrick (b. 1842), who was invited to the 'old palace' of Maharaja Chamarajendra of Mysore (r. 1868-94) in order to paint his children. In the Music Room she found that 'every chair I sat on played a different tune, lions roared by pulling their tails, automaton barristers gesticulated excitedly as if pleading their cause, wax clowns smoked cigarettes; it was a room to delight the heart of any child, and contained two beautiful organs and a tremolo piano.'[15] On visiting Jai Vilas Palace in Gwalior, the actress Yvonne Fitzroy (b. 1891) was similarly impressed by the ingenious mechanical works collected by the ruler. The Banqueting Hall was decorated with 'an electric rock garden', while 'tiny silver fountains played on the side tables', and 'the centre table was ingeniously lit with revolving coloured balls'. Around the dining table ran a miniature silver railway powered by electricity, and activated by a button accessible from the maharaja's seat (p. 163).[16] The goods carried by the train were after-dinner delectables: brandy, port, cigars, cigarettes, sweets, nuts and chocolates. The

carriages were sensitised, so that the train automatically stopped when a guest reached out for any of the contents!

No less sensational were the impressive mirrors, chandeliers and glass furniture that Indian princes commissioned from European firms. From the perspective of Western visitors, a profusion of sparkling chandeliers and looking-glasses was characteristic of an Indian palace interior.[17] In the 18th century various British firms took the lead in satisfying the Indian glass market, among them William Parker and Perry & Co. The activities of these firms were surpassed in the mid-to-late 19th century by businesses that established offices in India, such as F&C Osler (1840) and Baccarat (1896). The Osler archives yield considerable information about the way the firm captured the Indian market, including printing catalogues priced in rupees and producing Indian forms in glass such as *hookah* bases, fly whisks and *punkahs*.[18] The firm closely studied the local market, scouting for every possible opportunity to expand its sales. For instance, a letter of 1878 from Osler's Calcutta agent, Henry Pratt, reveals his desire to 'try to introduce native dinner sets in crockery', an idea based on the belief that in the modern age Hindus were gradually becoming inclined to reuse vessels even if not made of metal.[19] This idea resulted in the production by Osler of glass *thals* and finger-bowls.

Osler opened its own showroom in Calcutta in 1844, but the big business of supplying maharajas often depended on visits to princely states made by the firm's agents, who sold glass chandeliers, fountains and furniture principally through the designs they took with them (pp. 177-79).[20] As well as works from stock, Osler accepted special commissions, such as an extravagant glass fountain made for Maharaja Mahendra Singh of Patiala (r. 1862-76) in 1874, which was displayed in London before shipment to India. In 1884 the firm produced for an unnamed Indian prince a crystal throne 'believed to be the most important example of cut-glass that has ever been made'.[21] Dealing with princes was seldom straightforward. As one Osler agent found in Patiala, 'The Chief is not given to words to Englishmen but the aide-de-camp told me that two grunts & a shake of the hand which were all I got was to be considered highly satisfactory. All the talking is done afterwards.'[22] In this instance the ruler purchased a 104-light chandelier because 'he wanted a large centre chandelier in time for the Governor General's visit so he took it.'

143

144

FACING PAGE: Pair of plates, porcelain, painted with botanical specimens St Bruno's Lily (above) and Heron's Bill (below). Made by Chamberlain's Worcester for Nawab Azam Jah of Arcot, 1820-21. These plates belong to a substantial service ordered by the nawab on his accession through the Madras firm Griffiths, Cooke & Co. The plates carry a Persian inscription which translates to: 'Amir Al Hind Nawab Azam Jah Bahadur Hijri 1236'. The date corresponds to November 1820 - September 1821, but the service was not shipped to India until 1823.

Plate, porcelain. Made by Flight Barr and Barr for Nawab Ghazi-ud-din Haidar of Oudh, c. 1814-16. Before they were formally bestowed with coats of arms, Indian princes under western influence used their own emblems to simulate the effects of western heraldry, as is evident on the decoration of this plate. The ruler's initials NGH are flanked by twin fish, the symbol of Lucknow, and supported by a pair of tigers, all surmounted by a *katar* (punch dagger).

Richly Enamelled
Jeweller &
gilt to match
Service as
supplied to
H.M. The Queen

Maharajah of
Mahar Bhavnagar
Bhavnagar

		Each
Dinner plate		4.10.0
Cheese "		3.18.6
Soup Tld		25.0.0
Sauce Tld		15.0.0
Cover dish		15.0.0
Salad Bowl		12.12.0
Dish No 20		~~5.15.6~~ 14.14.
" 18		~~4.14.6~~ 12.12.0
" 16		~~3.10.0~~ 10.10.0
" 14		~~3.10.0~~ 8.8.0
" 12		~~4.4.0~~ 5.15.6
" 10		~~4.4.6~~ 4.14.6
Coffee Cup Sc		3.10.0
Tea " & Scr		3 10.
Slop		4.4..
Loaf		4.4..
Cream		3 3.
Muffin Cov		7.7.
Plate 5"		2.10.

Forward.

20/11/94

See Letter Mr Abraham
not only quoted
Mr + B nearly same price

RIGHT: Plate, porcelain. Made by Copeland for Maharaja Umaid Singh II of Kotah, early 20th century.

BOTTOM RIGHT: Designs for a monogram, ink and gouache on paper. By Thomas Goode & Co., for Maharaja Nripendra Narayan of Cooch Behar, 1885. Monograms and coats of arms were often a central component of the decoration of dinner services. Templates from the archives at Thomas Goode reveal that porcelain ordered by Maharaja Nripendra Narayan of Cooch Behar was decorated with his initial and a bee–a symbol of industry–surmounted by a coronet.

BOTTOM: Plate, porcelain. Made by Minton for Maharaja Vijaysinhji Chhatrasinhji of Rajpipla, early 20th century.

FACING PAGE: Order for a dinner service from Thomas Goode & Co., London, for Maharaja Takhtsinhji Jaswantsinhji of Bhavnagar, 1894. The firm's impressive Mayfair shop was much visited by Indian princes in London. Goode retailed porcelain from major British factories and specialised in commissions for dinner services.

147

Banquet held in the Durbar Hall, Laxmi Vilas Palace, Baroda on the occasion of a state visit of Maharaja Ganga Singh of Bikaner, 1934. In a speech of 1933 Gaekwar Sayajirao III declared that 'There is, perhaps, no finer room in India.'

149

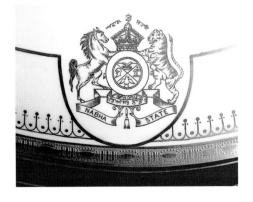

Pieces from a dinner service and detail of the Nabha coat of arms, porcelain. Made by Minton for Maharaja Ripudaman Singh of Nabha, c. 1920. The ruler is reputed to have entertained his British guests to a forty-two course dinner using this service.

FACING PAGE: Maharaja Pratap Singh of Nabha seated at a table set with the Minton dinner service ordered by his father, c. 1942.

152

ABOVE AND FACING PAGE TOP RIGHT: Pieces from a dinner service, porcelain. Made by W. Guerin & Cie. for Gaekwar Pratapsinhrao of Baroda, c. 1940.

FACING PAGE: List of orders from India, China and Japan, c. 1930. Thomas Goode & Co.'s international clients included many of the ruling houses of Europe and Asia.

I N D I A   C H I N A   &   J A P A N

EAST

	1	H.M. THE KING OF SIAM	G.D.E. with Crest in flat gold on rim.
	2	T. ASABUKI, ESQ.,	A.6098, turquoise festoons with Swastika Crest on rim in turq. & gold.
B.22	3	H.H. PRINCE CHAROON	1/9720, Chinese blossom design with snake style Crest in green in centre.
A.59	4	THE VICEROY OF INDIA	G.764, Turquoise & gold with Collar, star & Pendant in centre in p.c.
A.58	5	THE VICEROY OF INDIA	G.1210, Crimson & flower border with similar badge as above.
B.13	6	THE VICEROY OF INDIA	G.1214, Crimson & gold border with Star in centre
B.17	7	H.H. THE MAHARAJA OF RAJPIPLA	H.3563, yellow & black border with gold with Arms in p.c. on rim.
*	8	H.H. THE MAHARAJA OF RAJPIPLA	Yellow, black & gold bdr. with floral wreath with Arms in centre in p.c.
B.15	9	H.H. THE MAHARAJA OF KOLHAPUR, G.C.I.E.,	Yellow & gold with Crest on rim in p.c.
	10	H.H. THE MAHARAJA (Gaekwar) OF BARODA	1/7281 white & gold with Arms in raised gold in centre.
B.18	11	H.H. THE MAHARAJA (Gaekwar) OF BARODA	G.1214, Crimson & gold with Arms in centre in pc
B.21	12	H.H. THE MAHARAJA (Gaekwar) OF BARODA	G.2887, blue & gold with Arms in raised gold in centre.
B.20	13	H.I.M. THE SHAH OF PERSIA 1927	Ivory & gold with Crown in circle on rim in flat gold.
B.19	14	H.H. THE SULTAN OF SELANGOR	Ivory ground red border with Arms & motto in flat gold on rim.
*	15	H.R.H. PRINCE MAHIDOL	Stanley, gold edge with mono. in flat gold in centre.
B.16	16	H.H. THE MAHARAJA OF BIKANER	B.1005, Blue & flowers
B.14	17	H.H. MAJOR SIR UMAID SINGH, of Kotah	R.2231 Hamburg, green & gold with Arms in centre in p.c.

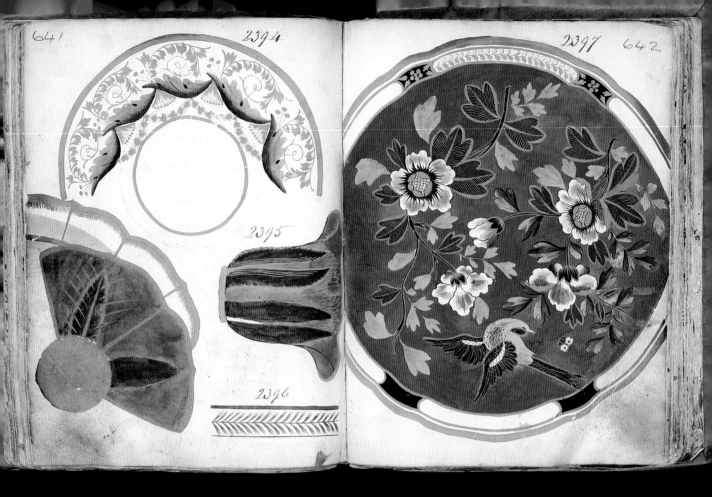

ABOVE: Tableware designs from a pattern book, gouache on paper. Spode, early 19th century. King Ghazi-ud-din Haidar of Oudh commissioned a service based on Pattern 2394, which was made for him c. 1820. The centre of each plate was decorated with his badge, consisting of a *katar* (punch dagger) flanked by twin fish and surmounted by a western-style pointed crown.

LEFT: Maharaja Ganga Singh of Bikaner during his visit to the Spode Factory showroom in Stoke, 1903.

FACING PAGE: Pages from a shape book, ink on paper. Spode, 1820. The range of wares produced at the factory included *hookah* bases intended for the Indian market. These technical diagrams were used in the production process, the thrower's measurements given on the left and the turner's on the right.

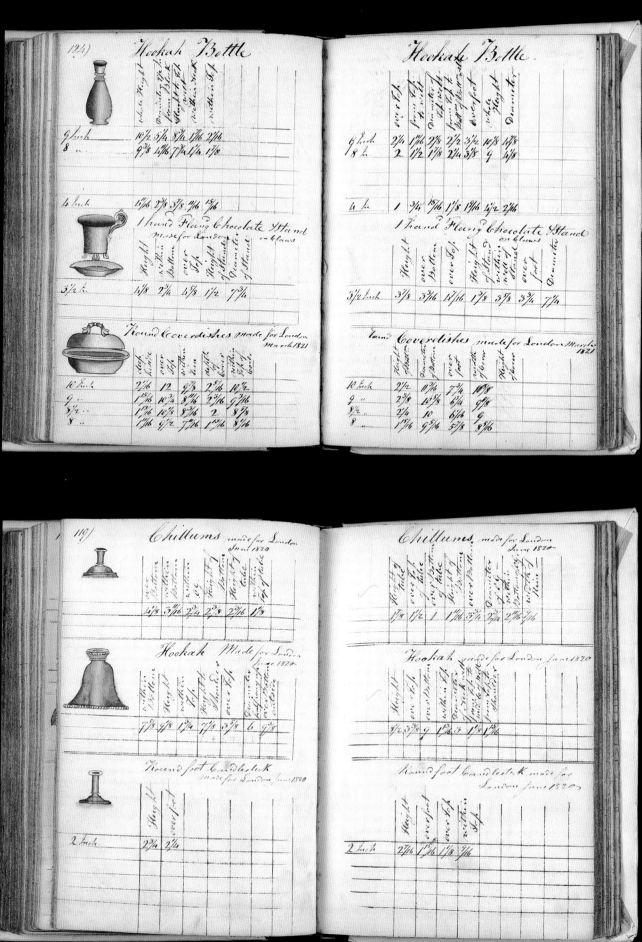

Hookah Bottle — Hookah Bottle

	whole Height	Diameter Bulb	Height Neck	within Neck	within Top		over Top	Proj: Top	Diameter over Top	Diameter Bottom Neck	over foot	whole Height	Quantity
9 inch	10½	5¼	8¾	1 7/16	2 2/16		2¼	1 7/16	2⅞	2½	3½	10⅞	1⅞
8 "	9⅞	4 9/16	7¾	1¼	1⅞		2	1½	1⅞	2¼	3⅜	9	4⅜
4 inch	15/16	2⅞	3⅜	4/16	15/16		1	¾	15/16	1⅞	19/16	4½	2 6/16

1 hand Fleuing Chocolate Stand made for London on Claws

	Height	within Bottom	over Top	Height of Stand	Diameter of Stand		Height	over Bottom	within Top	Height of Stand	within height of Stand	over foot	Quantity
5½ in	4⅛	2¾	4⅝	1½	7¾		3⅞	3 5/16	1 7/16	1⅞	3⅜	3¾	7¾

Round Coverdishes made for London March 1821

	each divide	over Top	within Top	height Cover	within Deep Cover		Height Bottom	Diameter of Bottom	over Top	within height Cover	Height Cover
10 inch	2 6/16	12	9⅜	2 5/16	10½		2½	10 7/16	7¾	10⅞	
9 "	1 15/16	10¾	8 11/16	2 5/16	9 7/16		2⅞	10⅝	6¾	9⅞	
8½ "	1¾	10⅛	8 5/16	2	8⅞		2¼	10	6 5/16	9	
8 "	1 7/16	9½	7 7/16	1 5/16	8 6/16		1 7/16	9 5/16	5⅞	8 5/16	

Chillums made for London June 1820 — Chillums made for London June 1820

over Bottom	within Bottom	within Top	Top	Height Bottom	Height Table	top of Table		Height of Table	over Top	over Bottom	Height Bottom	over Bottom	Diameter Top	within Bottom	Diameter of...	within of Table	width of Rim
4⅝	3 11/16	2¼	2⅜	2 6/16	1⅜			1⅞	1½	1	1 7/16	3 7/16	2¼	2 7/16	9/16		

Hookah Made for London June 1820 — Hookah made for London June 1820

within Bottom	Height	within Top	over Top	Height Shoulder	over Top	Diameter height Shoulder	Diameter of Bottom outside		Height	over Top	over Bottom	within Top	Diameter Top	height top of Shoulder	Diameter
7⅞	9⅛	1¾	7⅜	3⅜	6	9⅞			8½	3⅞	9	1 6/16	3	1¾	1 5/16

Round foot Candlestick made for London June 1820 — Round foot Candlestick made for London June 1820

	Height	over foot		Height	over foot	over Top	within Top
2 Inch	2¾	2¼		2 Inch	2 6/16	1 6/16	1⅛	9/16

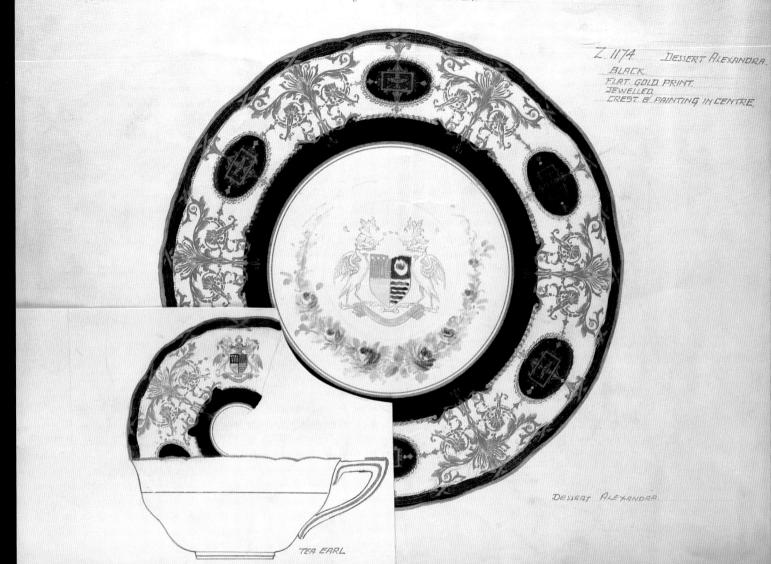

Tableware designs, gouache and pencil on paper. By Royal Worcester for Nawab Sadiq Muhammed Khan Abbasi V of Bahawalpur, 1933. 'Earl' and 'Alexandra' refer to standard shapes produced by the firm.

FACING PAGE: Pieces from a dinner service, porcelain. Made by Royal Worcester for Nawab Sadiq Muhammed Khan Abbasi V of Bahawalpur, 1933. The set was extensive and included services for breakfast, tea and coffee, as well as for a complete dinner sitting; the serving plates alone came in five different sizes.

FACING PAGE: Pieces from a dinner service, porcelain. Made by Royal Worcester for Gaekwar Pratapsinhrao of Baroda, 1947-48. The service was painted with a range of secular and spiritual images including courtly scenes and depictions of Hindu deities.

ABOVE: Paintings of Brahma, Radha and Krishna and a courtly lady pig-sticking, gouache on paper; and corresponding tea pot stands, porcelain (below). Made by Royal Worcester for Gaekwar Pratapsinhrao of Baroda, 1947-48.

159

DATE. 1923.   FOR H.R.H. PRINCE. RANJI SIN

Design for a desert plate, gouache on paper, and corresponding plate, from the 'English Scenes Service', porcelain. Made by Royal Worcester for Jam Saheb Ranjitsinhji of Nawanagar, design 1923; plate 1925. The plate belongs to a service painted by Harry Davis of scenes around the ruler's estate near Staines. Ranji used these plates while in Nawanagar as a reminder of his English home.

Design for a desert plate from the 'Indian Scenes Service', gouache on paper. By Royal Worcester for Jam Saheb Ranjitsinhji of Nawanagar, 1925. The design is for a plate from a set painted by Harry Davis of views of Jamnagar, the capital of Ranji's state, which he developed considerably. The plate depicts Kotha Bastion, near the Lakhota and Khambaliya Lakes. Ranji used these plates while in England as a reminder of his favourite spots at home.

Tantalus, glass, with gilt bronze. Made by Baccarat, 1877, exhibited at the Exposition Universelle, Paris, 1878 and purchased by Gaekwar Sayajirao III of Baroda. A locked set of decanters derives its name from Tantalus, a figure in Greek mythology who stole ambrosia and nectar from the table of Zeus, king of the gods. The elephant is inspired by the design of a fountain commissioned in 1808 by Napoleon from the architect Jean-Antoine Alavoine. The gilt bronze howdah is fitted with four engraved decanters and the harness supports twelve tumblers.

FACING PAGE: Miniature train, silver, with glass. Made by Armstrong Whitworth & Co. for Maharaja Jayaji Rao Scindia of Gwalior, early 20th century. The train is designed to circulate digestives and delectables among guests attending state dinners at Jai Vilas Palace, Gwalior. The lining of the silver carriages is sensitised so that the train stops as soon as a guest reaches out for any of the contents. The manufacturer was one of Britain's leading producers of armaments, locomotives and automobiles.

165

FACING PAGE TOP LEFT: Glasses, glass, blown, cut, engraved and painted in gold and enamel. Made by Baccarat for Gaekwar Sayajirao III of Baroda, probably 1925.

TOP RIGHT: Glass, glass, blown, moulded, engraved and gilt. Made by Baccarat for Gaekwar Pratapsinhrao of Baroda, 1947.

BOTTOM LEFT: Glass, glass, blown, cut, engraved and painted in gold and enamel. Made by Baccarat and purchased by Gaekwar Pratapsinhrao of Baroda, 1949.

BOTTOM RIGHT: Glass, glass, blown, cut and engraved. Made by Baccarat for Maharani Chimnabai II of Baroda, 1931.

LEFT: Decanter, glass, blown and engraved. Made by Baccarat for Maharaja Jagatjit Singh of Kapurthala, 1893.

RIGHT: Decanter, glass, blown, cut, engraved and painted in gold and enamel. Made by Baccarat for Gaekwar Pratapsinhrao of Baroda, 1949. Baccarat created this design, called 'Lagny' in 1908.

166

Part of a dinner service, silver-gilt. Made by the Goldsmiths and Silversmiths Company for Maharaja Bhupinder Singh of Patiala, 1921. The service was ordered by the maharaja in time for the visit to Patiala of Edward, Prince of Wales in 1922 and cost £30,000. The Goldsmiths and Silversmith Company was successful in securing the patronage of Indian princes, who regularly visited the company's impressive showrooms in Regent Street.

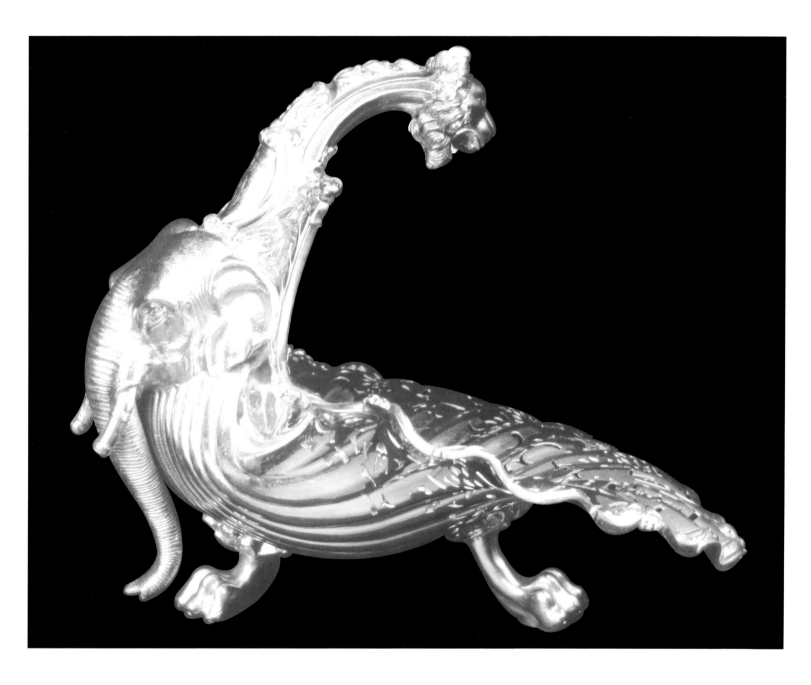

Dish, silver-gilt. Made by the Goldsmiths and Silversmiths Company for Maharaja Bhupinder Singh of Patiala, 1921. Although most of the service is based on western designs, some pieces reflect the Indian patron behind this extraordinary order.

168

Moustache spoon, silver. Made by Barton Silver, Bangalore and purchased by
Maharaja Ganga Singh of Bikaner, c. 1900. Soup spoons with guards came into
use in the last quarter of the 19th century and were driven by the male fashion
for wearing a moustache. They were designed so that men could drink their soup
without leaving any traces behind. This piece was made by a British firm in
Bangalore and bears the maharaja's initials 'GS'.

Maharaja Ganga Singh of Bikaner by Herzog and Higgins, 1912.

RIGHT: Sauce boat, silver. Made by Roberts and Belk, Sheffield, 1930-31 and purchased by Maharaja Ganga Singh of Bikaner.

Spoon, silver. Made by James Dixon and Sons, Sheffield, 1924-25 and purchased by Maharaja Ganga Singh of Bikaner.

BELOW: Advertisement for the Goldsmiths and Silversmiths Company, Ltd., c. 1920. The firm concentrated on capturing the market for English silver in India, partly achieved through an active advertising policy. The company's shop in Regent Street was lavishly decorated, with a separate showroom devoted to silver for the colonial market.

FACING PAGE TOP: Boat, glass with gilt bronze. Made by Baccarat, 1900, displayed by Le Grand Dépôt at the Exposition Universelle, Paris 1900; bought by Maharaja Ganga Singh of Bikaner in 1930. The boat is based on a design by Charles Vital Cornu (1851-1927). Baccarat made two glass boats of this type, with minor variations in the modelling of the figures. The second example is now in the collection of the Corning Museum of Glass, New York.

FACING PAGE BOTTOM: Glass boat, gouache and watercolour on paper, c. 1900. The image is perhaps a proposed design for the two glass boats made by Baccarat. In the completed works the figure at the head of the boat is not blowing a horn.

Pair of vases, porcelain, painted with the portraits of Maharaja Jagatjit Singh and Rani Kanari of Kapurthala, French, c. 1886. According to tradition these vases were ordered by the ruler on his first marriage. The portraits were based on photographs provided to the unidentified manufacturer. The maharaja is shown wearing a tiara over his turban, while his wife is depicted wearing an elaborate diamond hairpiece.

Elephant Mystery Clock, gold, platinum, jade, onyx, rock crystal, mother-of-pearl, pearls, coral, diamonds and black enamel. Made by Cartier, 1928; the jade elephant Chinese, 18th century; purchased by Jam Saheb Ranjitsinhji of Nawanagar. The allure of this piece lies not only in its exotic design and its rare materials, but also in its technical wizardry. The arms of the clock are set against a transparent dial and appear to be floating. The movement is mysteriously concealed, enhancing the viewer's sense of wonder.

Gravity Clock, gold, lapis lazuli, malachite, cornelian, turquoise, mother-of-pearl, coral, emerald, diamond and blue enamel. Made by Cartier, 1927 and purchased by Maharaja Bhupinder Singh of Patiala. The clock is ingeniously designed so that the face slides down the shaft as the hours pass.

173

174

Bed, rosewood, encrusted with silver, the figures of bronze. Made by Christofle for Nawab Muhammad Bahawal Khan Abbasi V of Bahawalpur, 1882-83. The four figures at the corners represent women of France, Spain, Italy and Greece. Through ingenious mechanics the statues were capable of winking and waving the fans and fly whisks in their hands. It was perhaps the suggestive character of the bed that led the nawab to safeguard his anonymity; Christofle discovered that he was the client behind this extraordinary commission only in 1983.

LEFT: Detail of the footboard.

Bed, gouache on paper, 1883. To add to its other attributes, the bed
was fitted with a music box which played a thirty minute interlude
from Gounod's *Faust*, activated by a button. This painting was made
before the bed was dispatched to India.

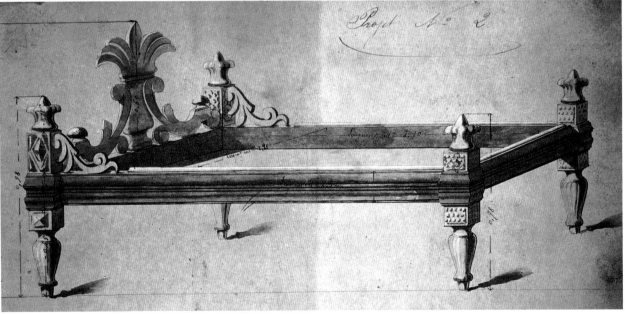

176

Two designs for a glass bed, pencil with gouache on paper. By Baccarat, 1879. These designs cannot be identified with any particular client; it is likely that they were devised simply as stock pieces for Baccarat's Bombay showroom, which opened in 1883 to meet the growing local demand for glass furniture and lighting. Among the firm's exceptional Indian commissions is a crystal tombstone ordered by an unnamed Indian prince in 1930.

FACING PAGE: Design for a glass bedstead from a design book, ink and gouache on paper. By F&C Osler, 1883. Osler established a showroom in Calcutta in 1844 in which were displayed both stock models and wares produced specifically for the Indian market such as *hookah* bases, *punkah* poles and *chowries* (fly whisks). The firm's agents in India regularly visited princely states, where they sought special commissions. This bed is typical of the kind of furniture made for Indian princes; a related example is in the Crystal Gallery, Fateh Prakash Palace, Udaipur.

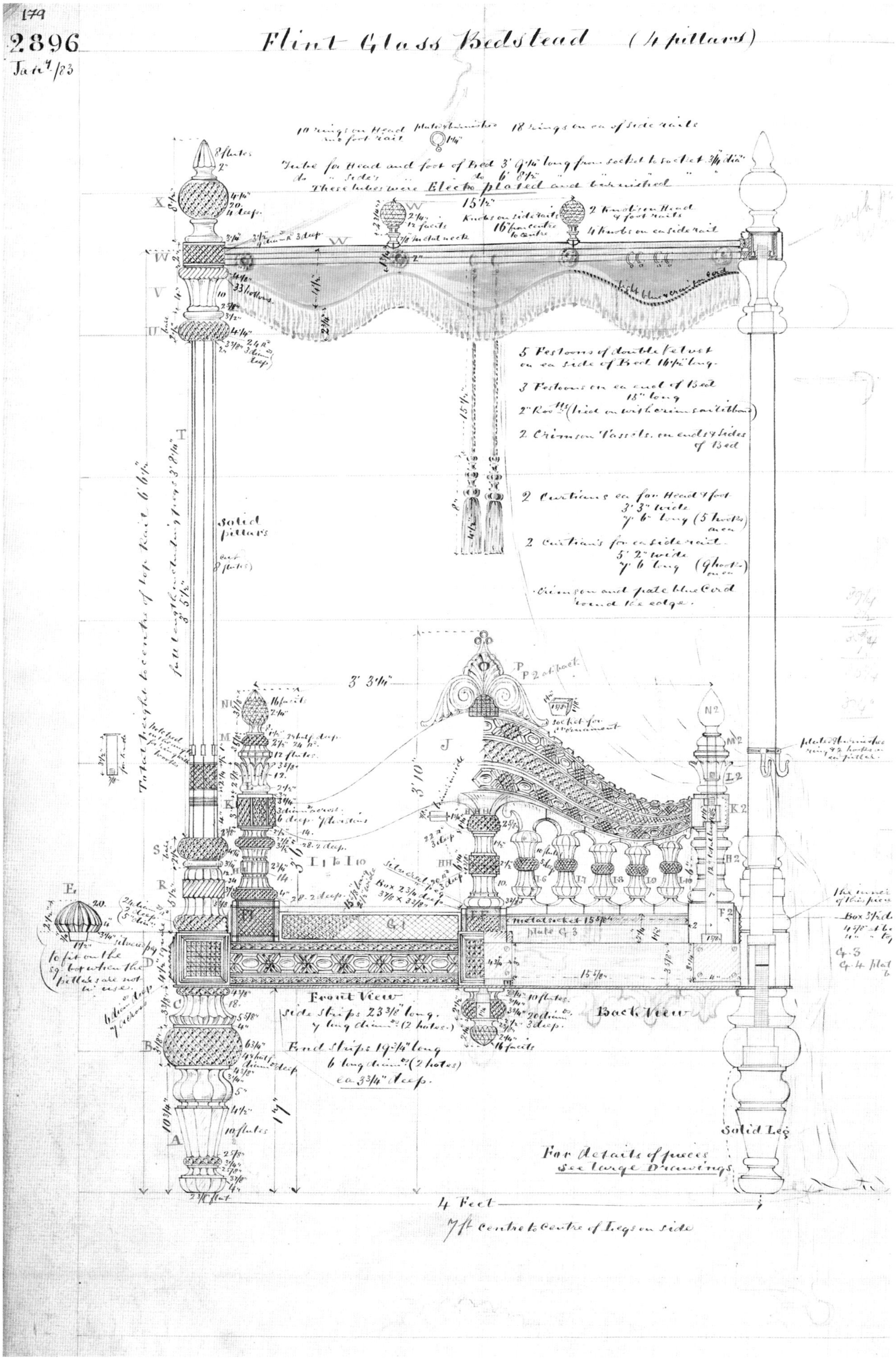
179
2896
Jan 4/83
Flint Glass Bedstead (4 pillars)
These tubes were Electro plated and burnished
5 Festoons of double velvet on ea side of Bed 16½" long.
3 Festoons on ea end of Bed 18" long
2 Crimson Tassels on ends & sides of Bed
2 Curtains ea for Head & foot 3' 3" wide 7' 6" long (5 hooks on ea)
2 Curtains for ea side rail 5' 2" wide 7' 6" long (9 hooks on ea)
Crimson and pale blue Cord round the edge.
solid pillars
Front View
Back View
Side strips 23⅜" long
End strips 19¼" long
Solid Leg
For details of pieces see large Drawings
4 Feet
7 ft centre to centre of Legs on side

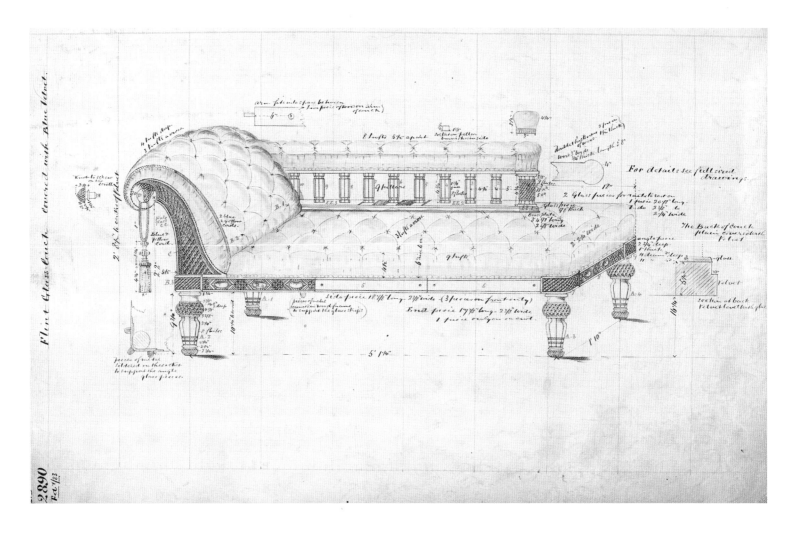

178

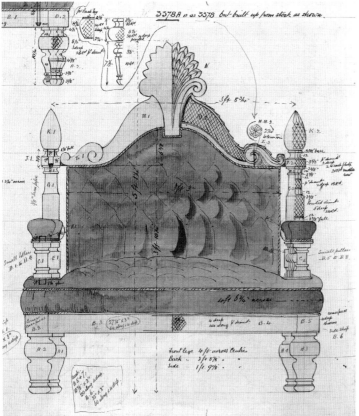

ABOVE: Design for a glass chaise longue from a design book, ink and gouache on paper. By F&C Osler, 1883.

LEFT: Design for a glass settee from a design book, ink and gouache on paper. By F&C Osler, early 20th century.

These technical drawings were used by Osler workmen in the execution of the designs at hand. Drawings–and later, photographs–were illustrated in Osler's catalogues.

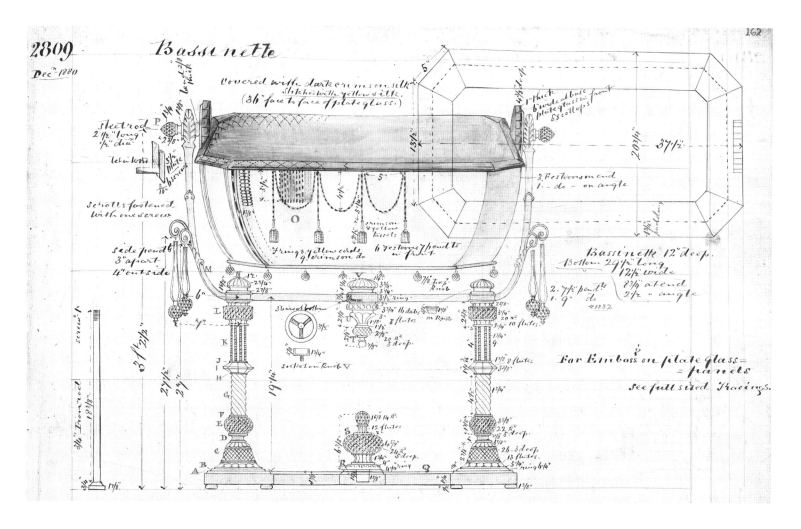

ABOVE: Design for a glass bassinet from a design book, ink and gouache on paper. By F&C Osler, 1880. This piece was part of a substantial commission from Nawab Muhammad Bahawal Khan Abbasi V of Bahawalpur.

LEFT: Crystal Gallery, Fateh Prakash Palace, Udaipur. English-speaking Maharana Sajjan Singh of Udaipur placed his first order from Osler in 1878, at the age of nineteen. In 1881 and 1882 the ruler commissioned further pieces, which were intended as the principal decoration for palace apartments then under construction. His untimely death in 1884 deprived the maharana of the pleasure of receiving these orders, which were later complimented by works from Osler bought by his successors. These are now displayed collectively in the Fateh Prakash Palace, Udaipur.

LEFT: Design for a glass fountain, pencil, ink and watercolour on paper. By Baccarat, 1861.

RIGHT: Fountain, glass. Made by F&C Osler and acquired by Maharana Sajjan Singh of Udaipur, c. 1878. The fountain was a stock model sold extensively by the firm from its Calcutta showrooms. This example was probably acquired by the ruler as part of his first order in 1878.

FACING PAGE: Design for a standing candelabrum, ink on tracing paper. By Leopold William Jones for an unnamed Indian prince, c. 1870. The design is inscribed 'Candelabra for 50 Wax Light For the Durbar Hall Finest British Quality'.

No. 4

Candelabra
for 50 Wax Lights

For The Durbar
Hall.

Finest British Quality

ROYAL PURSUITS

❦

'THE MAHARAJA [OF PATIALA] LOVED LIFE AND FOOD
AND WOMEN AND JEWELS, BUT BECAUSE HE WAS
SO SPLENDID AND RICH, SO EXTRAVAGANT, SO
GENEROUS AND HOSPITABLE, BECAUSE HE SHOT WELL
AND DROVE HIS ENORMOUS CARS AT A FANTASTIC
PACE AND STOPPED THEM AT ONCE IF THE POOREST
OF HIS SUBJECTS WANTED TO TALK TO HIM, BECAUSE
HE LAUGHED AND SCATTERED MONEY INTO THE
HANDS OF BEGGARS, HIS PEOPLE WERE
GENUINELY ATTACHED TO HIM.'

Rosita Forbes, *India of the Princes*, 1939.

FACING PAGE: Princess Harshad Kumari with her father, Jam Saheb Digvijaysinhji of Nawanagar, c. 1939. This car was custom-made for the young princess but when admired by the young prince of Jaipur, Bhawani Singh, it was given to him as a birthday present.

As rulers, princes were meant to personify power, showing strength and physical courage in warfare and in the protection of their people. Under the Raj, maharajas exercised their talents in warfare on behalf of the British Empire, in both active and honorific positions. Princes also demonstrated physical prowess through sport, in hunting expeditions and games that illustrated their dexterity and their skills in horsemanship and shooting. Power was also an implicit aspect of the princely passion for motor cars. The new technology behind car travel was exciting, symbolising modernity and westernisation. Automobiles themselves were luxury machines, and enhanced the prestige of their owners. The thrill of modern travel was captured above all by the aeroplane, which offered new opportunities for adventure and recreation. In India, maharajas were at the forefront of the transport revolution, possessing before others the exciting new technologies that transformed travel and communication.

Sport, whether polo, tennis or cricket provided a point of mutual contact and camaraderie between Indian princes and the Europeans they encountered. *Shikar* or hunting in particular, became a highly public form of recreation in which rulers and their guests demonstrated their mastery over fierce animals, above all, tigers. During his visit to India in 1922-23, Edward, Prince of Wales (1894-1972) and his party were hosted successively by the rulers of Mysore, Gwalior, Bhopal, Jodhpur, Patiala, Baroda, Bikaner and Bharatpur, who treated them to the best sport available in their lands, including big-game hunting and pig-sticking as well as shooting duck, black buck and grouse.[1] The ritual of these sports relied on high-quality weapons made by western gun and rifle manufacturers. These could be purchased through agents in India such as Army & Navy Stores, or commissioned directly from the makers themselves. Maharajas constituted an important client base for companies such as Holland and Holland, Remington and Purdeys and were responsible for extravagant commissions, developing extensive armouries. Many of the guns made for Indian princes by Holland and Holland 'were highly engraved, inlaid with precious metals and housed in cases of extraordinary quality'(p. 200).[2] Some princes, like Maharaja Jai Singh of Alwar (r. 1892-1937), had particular requests. As a strict Hindu, he demanded that his gun-cases be of oak or canvas rather than leather. Trophies from hunting expeditions were routinely preserved by European taxidermists in India, among them Van Igen & Van Ingen, and

installed in palace interiors. Far more stylish, Maharani Indira Devi of Cooch Behar (1892-1968), commissioned renowned couturier Elsa Schiaparelli (1890-1973) to create a carpet from fourteen tiger-skins![3] On her visit to Dholpur, artist Emily Merrick (b. 1842) was much impressed by the sporting trophies of the ruler of the state, Maharaj Rana Nihal Singh (r. 1873-1901): 'The room where I was received had the floor and couches covered with handsome skins of lions, tigers, bears, white leopards, and silver foxes, the chief ornaments consisting of silver cups and bowls, some very handsome, won by the Maharajah for shooting, polo, pig-sticking, and racing, for he is an excellent sportsman.'[4]

Some princes also took pleasure in keeping animals, either as pets, for sporting, or indeed as livestock. Horses and dogs were routinely imported to India. More unusual is an account of Gaekwar Pratapsinhrao of Baroda's (r. 1939-51) consignment from Europe of dogs, cats, grouse and other poultry in January 1956. There was no guarantee that animals could withstand the long journey from England to India and in this instance one of the hens, reported as 'off colour and not taking food and water since the vessel left Port Said' died and was confined to the deep (p. 198).[5] An unnamed Indian prince was so devoted to a pet tree frog that he commissioned Van Cleef & Arpels to create a golden terrarium for it.[6] Named 'La Maison d' Hortense', presumably after the pet, the frog-house is a tour-de-force of 1930s design and craftsmanship (p. 198). Nawab Mahabat Khan III of Junagadh (r. 1911-59) was similarly generous towards his pet dogs, who were given splendid collars emblazoned with the ruler's arms. The nawab's affection for his favourite bitch, Roshanara, extended to arranging a marriage for her to Bobby, a golden retriever belonging to the nawab of Mangrol. In keeping with tradition, the bride was carried to the wedding in a silver palanquin in just one of the many ceremonies which took place over three days. The ninety-five dogs of Maharaja Bhupinder Singh of Patiala (r. 1900-38) were equally pampered by three English grooms and were lodged in 'wonderful' accommodation; the dog clinic at Patiala was considered finer than many hospitals in India.[7]

Cars were another ruling passion for mahajaras, some of whom became leading patrons of European automobile manufacturers. Like palanquins and carriages before them, cars were visible indicators of rank, and in appearance were designed to reflect the elevated status of their princely owners. Coats of arms on the doors, pennants and flags on the bonnet and distinctive license plates were all critical in enhancing the impression created by motor cars (pp. 212-13). As with other luxury goods from the west, it was the maharajas of Patiala who took the lead in automobiles, importing in 1898 a model from the French firm de Dion-Bouton, at that time Europe's leading car producer.[8] Apparently four cars of this type came to India at the same time, one for Rajinder Singh of Patiala (r. 1876-1900), Krishnaraja IV of Mysore (r. 1894-1940) and Mir Mahboob Ali Khan, Nizam of Hyderabad (r. 1869-1911), and one for Lord Curzon, Viceroy from 1899-1904.[9] Poor roads, frequent breakdowns and high cost did not dampen the princely appreciation of motor vehicles. Rather, as status symbols, cars were incorporated into royal ceremony and ritual, and given as dowries and extravagant wedding presents. Maharajas purchased cars in quantity; the fleet of the maharajas of Mysore, for instance, contained twenty-four Bentleys and Rolls-Royces alone.[10]

Although princes ordered many stock models, they were also responsible for a number of special commissions which are legends in automobile history. For instance, because he considered it inappropriate for a ruler to appear on the same level as his staff, Osman Ali Khan, Nizam of Hyderabad (r. 1911-67), commissioned from Barker and Company a car with a special elevated rear seat.[11] Maharana Bhupal Singh of Udaipur (r. 1930-55) overcame this obstacle by simply having his aide-de-camp squat on the car floor.[12] Jai Singh of Alwar anticipated the role of cars in royal processions and commissioned a Lanchester that was modelled on the British Coronation Coach.[13] Krishnaraja IV of Mysore commissioned a Ford saloon, half of which was 'a Hindu place of worship' and the other half 'a bath in which the Maharaja makes his ablutions'.[14] Piety was also the driving force behind the special cow-guards mounted on cars used by the royal family of Bharatpur.[15] So devout was Jai Singh of Alwar that the interiors of his cars were lined with French tapestry rather than leather.[16] It was only fitting that Indian princely cars should be embellished with the highest quality materials. A nizam of Hyderabad apparently ordered a Rolls-Royce with a silver body.[17] One of Gaekwar Sayajirao III of Baroda's (r. 1875-1939) cars had 24 carat gold-plated interior fittings, while a Rolls-Royce Phantom III ordered by his successor, Pratapsinhrao, was lined entirely in panther skin.[18] Some cars belonging to the Patiala royal family were finished with gold-plated dashboards and instruments set with precious stones.[19]

Automobile companies also routinely designed purdah cars with darkened windows and blinds so that women from the zenana could be transported with their modesty unimpaired. Cars were also specially designed for *shikar*. A ruler of Bharatpur ordered from Rolls-Royce a car with a sliding roof, designed for shooting tiger.[20] Bhupinder Singh of Patiala commissioned an Isotta Faschini Tipo 8A painted entirely in camouflage, and Nawab Hamidullah Khan of Bhopal (r. 1926-60) ordered a Bentley for hunting trips that was fitted with compartments for weapons, a locker for cartridges, and a trunk for picnic baskets, ice chests and flasks.[21] Maharaja Yeshwant Rao Holkar II of Indore (r. 1926-61) brought together motor vehicles and tents to create a Modernist mobile *shikar* caravan composed of the hold of four lorries–each of which turned into a room–around a central octagonal tented chamber (p. 223). By contrast, Bhupinder Singh of Patiala embarked on *shikar* expeditions with two Leyland buses that acted as dining rooms for his entourage.[22]

With the introduction of railways princes also commissioned luxurious private carriages, which were usually made in the west and finished in India. Among the finest of these was the railway car designed by Eckart Muthesius (1905-1989) for Yeshwant Rao II of Indore, which married a beautifully-styled chrome and glass interior with the latest technology, including air conditioning (p. 222). Toy railways and miniature electric cars were also in vogue for royal children. In Baroda, Gaekwar Pratapsinhrao (r. 1939-51) presented a toy train to his son Ranjitsinhrao (b. 1938) for travelling from Laxmi Vilas to the palace school (pp. 220-21). With advancements in air travel, some princes also developed an interest in flying. Among these were Maharaja Umaid Singh of Jodhpur (r. 1918-47), a collector of aeroplanes and an aviator himself, who happily dispatched planes to collect friends for parties (p. 195)! The maharaja established the Jodhpur Flying Club in 1931 and developed the airport at Jodhpur to the extent that it became a critical refuelling and maintenance centre for international flights. Yeshwant Rao Holkar II of Indore was also fond of aeroplanes and with typical attention to styling commissioned Muthesius to design the interiors of the two aeroplanes he purchased from Airspeed Ltd. The sleek finish epitomises luxury travel in the jet age (p. 224).

Regular travel and hunting expeditions required luggage, for which princes turned to leading European firms. Maharaja Hari Singh of Jammu and Kashmir (r. 1925-61) was a particularly good client, ordering from Louis Vuitton a suite of luggage initialed 'J&K' that included suitcases and wardrobes, a shoe case, a dressing box, a travelling case for a dictaphone and a travelling polo kit (pp. 186-87, 190-91 & 193). From Hermès he ordered sixty picnic baskets, as gifts for friends! Harrods also supplied the prince with beautifully monogrammed and crested wooden boxes for trout which he sent as presents in fishing season.[23] In 1930 Bhupinder Singh of Patiala provided Asprey's with a memorable commission: a set of teak trunks lined and fitted with solid silver washing and bathing equipment, including basins and bowls, soap boxes and tooth-brush holders. The ruler ordered five examples: one for each of his wives![24]

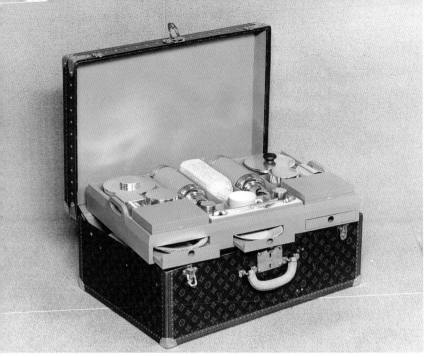

TOP: Lunch case, monogram canvas, ceramic and silver. Made by Louis Vuitton for Maharaja Hari Singh of Jammu and Kashmir, 1931.

BOTTOM: Special trunk for glass jars, monogram canvas. Made by Louis Vuitton for Maharaja Hari Singh of Jammu and Kashmir, 1931.

TOP: Special trunk for shoe and linen cleaning kit, monogram canvas. Made by Louis Vuitton for Maharaja Hari Singh of Jammu and Kashmir, 1931.

BOTTOM: Special desk wardrobe, monogram canvas. Made by Louis Vuitton for Maharaja Hari Singh of Jammu and Kashmir, 1928.

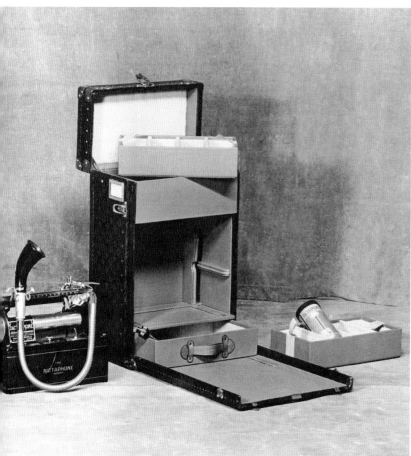

TOP LEFT AND RIGHT: Auto trunk (closed and open), vuittonite. Made by Louis Vuitton for Maharani Chimnabai II of Baroda, 1930.

BOTTOM LEFT: Special trunk for a dictaphone, monogram canvas. Made by Louis Vuitton for Maharaja Hari Singh of Jammu and Kashmir, 1928.

BOTTOM RIGHT: Secretaire for pharmaceuticals, vuittonite. Made by Louis Vuitton for Maharaja Hari Singh of Jammu and Kashmir, 1928.

By the early 20th century overseas travel was an integral part of Indian princely life. Famous for the beauty of their designs, the Parisian firm of Louis Vuitton was chosen by maharajas to execute their orders for trunks and custom-designed luggage, used to transport precious gifts and possessions from India to Europe and back.

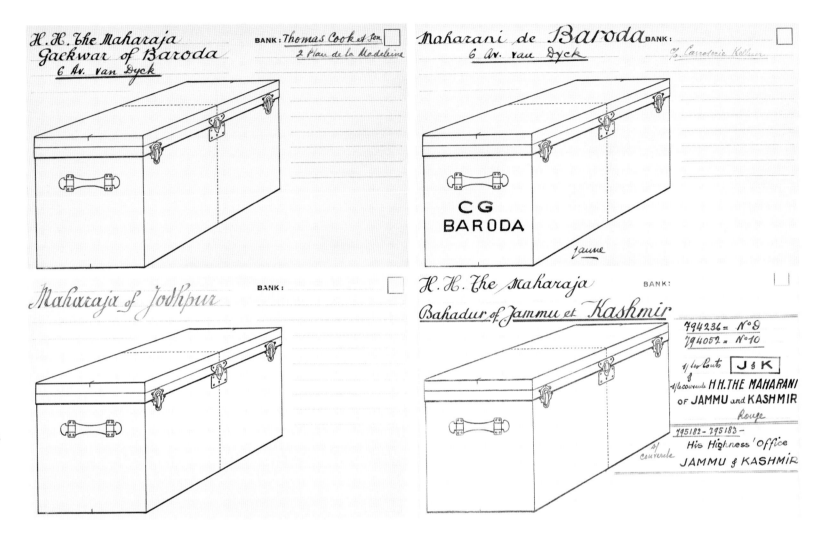

188

TOP: Customer cards, card with ink and pencil. By Louis Vuitton, early 20th century. These cards were used to keep record of special orders and included the clients' names and addresses. The luggage outlines were used to indicate how and where clients wished to represent their monogram or coat of arms. These particular cards were made for orders received from Maharaja Sayajirao III of Baroda, Maharani Chimnabai II of Baroda, Maharaja Umaid Singh of Jodhpur and Maharaja Hari Singh of Jammu and Kashmir.

LEFT AND ABOVE: Trunk, monogram canvas. Made by Louis Vuitton for Maharaja Jagatjit Singh of Kapurthala, 1938. The Francophile ruler was among Louis Vuitton's most significant Indian patrons. This piece is one from a set that included wardrobes, hat boxes and shoe trunks.

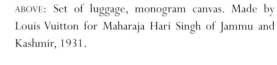

ABOVE: Set of luggage, monogram canvas. Made by Louis Vuitton for Maharaja Hari Singh of Jammu and Kashmir, 1931.

BELOW: Case for a typewriter, monogram canvas. Made by Louis Vuitton for Maharaja Hari Singh of Jammu and Kashmir, 1931.

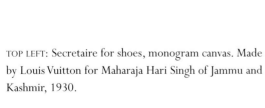

TOP LEFT: Secretaire for shoes, monogram canvas. Made by Louis Vuitton for Maharaja Hari Singh of Jammu and Kashmir, 1930.

ABOVE: Special trunk for shoes, monogram canvas. Made by Louis Vuitton for Maharaja Hari Singh of Jammu and Kashmir, 1930.

ABOVE: Maharaja Hari Singh of Jammu and Kashmir with Bobby Breward, 1931. Bobby Breward, salesman at Hermès in Cannes, was appointed to look after orders from the maharaja, who was a regular client. In this photograph Breward mounts an Hermès saddle on one of Hari Singh's horses.

LEFT: Picnic case, leather with silver and glass. Made by Hermès for Maharaja Hari Singh of Jammu and Kashmir, c. 1930. The ruler apparently ordered sixty such cases, to distribute as presents among his friends.

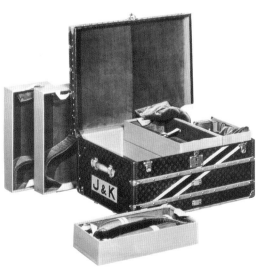

RIGHT: Trunk for polo equipment, monogram canvas. Made by Louis Vuitton for Maharaja Hari Singh of Jammu and Kashmir, 1931.

192

Tea case, long-grained leather, with silver, ceramic and glass. Made
by Louis Vuitton for Maharaja Sayajirao III of Baroda, 1926.

Tea case, leather, ceramic and silver. Made by Louis Vuitton for
Maharaja Hari Singh of Jammu and Kashmir, 1928.

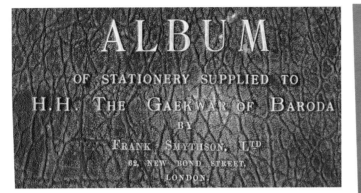

ALBUM
OF STATIONERY SUPPLIED TO
H.H. THE GAEKWAR OF BARODA
BY
FRANK SMYTHSON, LTD
82, NEW BOND STREET,
LONDON.

Princess Vimalaraje Gaekwar of Baroda
requests the pleasure of
Company at _____ on
the ___ of ___ at ___ o'clock

R.S.V.P.to
the Secretary to
Maharaj Kumar Dhairyashilrao Gaekwar.

Laxmi Vilas Palace.
Baroda.

Prince Dhairyshilrao Gaekwar.

Baroda.

Prince Jaisinh Gaekwar.

PRINCE DHAIRYASHIL,
GAEKWAR
OF BARODA.

*The Maharaja Gaekwar of Baroda
sends Greetings & Best Wishes for
Christmas & the New Year.*
*Laxmi Vilas Palace.
Baroda.*

*His Highness
Maharaja Sayaji Rao Gaekwar,*
of Baroda.

Selection of stationery, paper, die-stamped with hand-engraved dies. Made by Frank Smythson Ltd., for Gaekwar Sayajirao III of Baroda and family, 1920-30. The Baroda Christmas card features a photograph of the family seat, Laxmi Vilas Palace. On the various examples of letterhead the Baroda arms are set with mother-of-pearl, adding a touch of richness to the paper. Smythson remains London's foremost stationers.

ALBUM

OF STATIONERY SUPPLIED TO

H. H. THE MAHARAJA OF JODHPUR

BY

FRANK SMYTHSON LTD.

54, NEW BOND STREET,
LONDON.

Nearest Airport Jodhpur

Will you fly

to Sherry & Cocktails with us

on   at

(Air conditions permitting)

Jodhpur.

The Maharajah of Jodhpur
sends Greetings & Best Wishes
for Christmas and the New Year

Jodhpur,
Rajputana,
India.

MAYFAIR 8860
TELEGRAMS: CLARIDGES LONDON

Claridge's
Brook Street, W.1

Her Highness the Maharani of Jodhpur
at Home

on _____ at

Cocktails

Selection of stationery, paper, die-stamped with hand-engraved dies.
Made by Frank Smythson Ltd., for Maharaja Umaid Singh of Jodhpur
and family, c. 1925. The Jodhpur family Christmas card reflects the
maharaja's keen passion for flying, as does the invitation to drinks,
which offers guests air transport!

196 Selection of stationery, paper, die-stamped with hand-engraved dies. Made by Frank Smythson Ltd., for Maharani Sunity Devi and Maharani Indira Devi of Cooch Behar and Maharaja Man Singh II of Jaipur, 1920-30. The three bookplates (above) feature the names of different Jaipur properties.

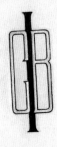

Woodlands,
Alipore,
Calcutta.

Selection of stationery, paper, die-stamped. Made by Appay for
Maharaja Jagatjit Singh of Kapurthala, c. 1900. The Persian script
translates to 'Maharaja Jagatjit Singh of Kapurthala'. The Francophile
ruler ordered his stationery from Paris.

CHÂTEAU KAPURTHALA
MUSSOORIE

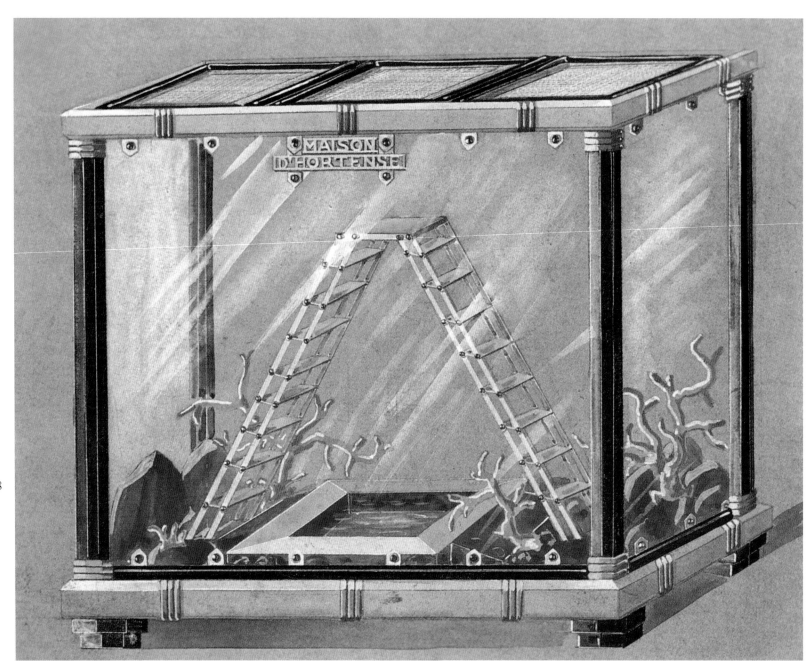

ABOVE: 'Maison D'Hortense', gold, coral, lapis lazuli, onyx and glass. Made by Van Cleef & Arpels for an unnamed Indian prince, 1935. This extraordinary commission, a house for a tree frog made of precious materials, was ordered by an Indian prince through a French agent, M. Delpierre. The frog apparently indicated changes in the weather by mounting or descending the golden ladder.

LEFT: Letter concerning the death of a hen imported to India by Gaekwar Pratapsinhrao of Baroda, 1956.

FACING PAGE: Letter regarding the importation of pets and poultry to Baroda by Gaekwar Pratapsinhrao, 1956.

Bombay 10th, February 1956.

MORTALITY CERTIFICATE.

Certified that one hen consigned to H.H. the Maharaja of Gaekwar of Baroda, was off colour and not taking food and water since the vessel left Port Said on 20/1/56. This hen died at noon on 21/1/56, and was confined to the deep.

Commander.

28th April 8

URGENT.

The Chief Controller of Imports & Exports,
New Delhi.

        Re: Import Licence/CCP No.0 048567/55/C.C.I./
           H.Q.dated 9-11-55.

        Ref:Your No.L-I B/H.H./17/2-55/96 dated
           7-9-56.

Sir,

        His Highness the Maharaja Saheb of Baroda
had placed an order for 7 dogs, one cat and poultry in
U.K. for which an import permit was obtained from you.

        The dogs and the cat arrived in Delhi by the
British Overseas Airways Corporation Service on 10-12-55
while the poultry arrived in Bombay by S.S.Itinda in
February 1956.

        As the actual value of the consignment
exceeded the amount of Rs.4940/- mentioned in the original
import licence and as the period of the validity of the
licence was required to be extended, a request was made
by His Highness under No.2539/5-3-56 for increasing the
value to Rs.10,000/- as well as for the extension of the
validity of the licence.

        The original licence, which was to follow
the above letter, got misplaced somehow and subsequently
a duplicate copy of the original licence with increased
value was obtained from you under your office letter
indicated in the reference. The said duplicate copy of
the licence is enclosed herewith.

        The cat and the dogs which had arrived at
Delhi were got cleared against the duplicate copy of the
licence but the poultry which came later at Bombay was
got cleared by depositing Rs. 1339/ with the Bombay
Customs office.

        Our agents Messrs.Asiatic Travel Service
Ltd., Bombay approached the Bombay Customs Authorities
for obtaining refund of Rs.1339/- by furnishing them a
copy of the duplicate licence. They were told that the
value left for utilisation was only about Rs.433 whereas
the value of the poultry imported was Rs.1339. The Customs
authorities in Bombay,therefore insist on this value being
amended or a licence to cover this amount be submitted to
to them. (copy enclosed)

        I shall therefore thank you to send me an
amended licence accordingly or to furnish us with a new
licence covering the value of the poultry,whichever is
suitable for you to arrange.

        An early action is solicited in the matter.

                    Yours faithfully

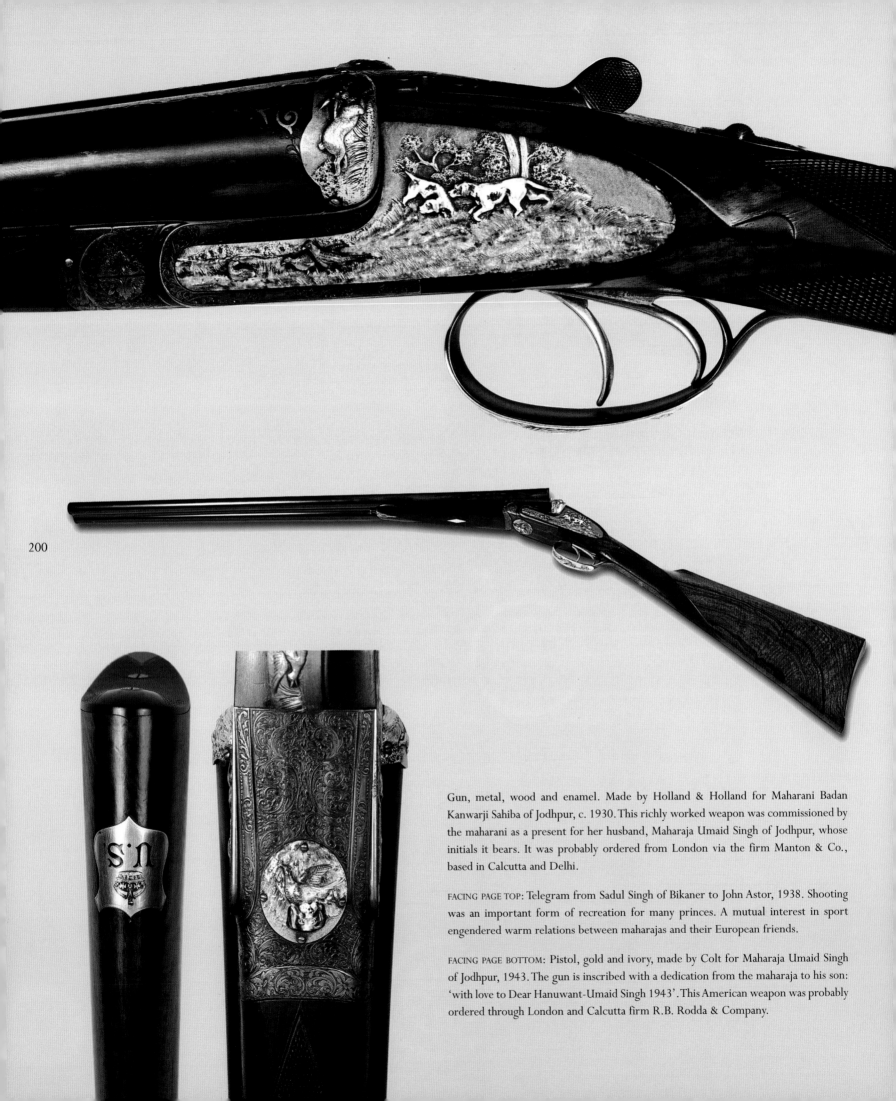

200

Gun, metal, wood and enamel. Made by Holland & Holland for Maharani Badan Kanwarji Sahiba of Jodhpur, c. 1930. This richly worked weapon was commissioned by the maharani as a present for her husband, Maharaja Umaid Singh of Jodhpur, whose initials it bears. It was probably ordered from London via the firm Manton & Co., based in Calcutta and Delhi.

FACING PAGE TOP: Telegram from Sadul Singh of Bikaner to John Astor, 1938. Shooting was an important form of recreation for many princes. A mutual interest in sport engendered warm relations between maharajas and their European friends.

FACING PAGE BOTTOM: Pistol, gold and ivory, made by Colt for Maharaja Umaid Singh of Jodhpur, 1943. The gun is inscribed with a dedication from the maharaja to his son: 'with love to Dear Hanuwant-Umaid Singh 1943'. This American weapon was probably ordered through London and Calcutta firm R.B. Rodda & Company.

TÉLÉGRAMME

POUR

INDICATIONS DE TRANSMISS

N°

Taxe principale

Mots

Taxes accessoires

Mentions de Service NON TAXÉES à transmettre au préambule

à   h   Total .. ..

John Astar

18 Carlton House Terrace

London

Many thanks delighted shoot ~~to de~~ Grouse August twentyfirst but not permitted do stiff walking as will shortly after tonsil operation Writing

Maharajkumar Bikaner

Nom et adresse de l'Expéditeur : Kalep Singh Asstt Secyto H.H. the Prince of Bikaner

(Ces indications ne sont taxées et transmises que sur la demande de l'Expéditeur)

27   5   30   Hotel Meurice, Paris.

Row of eight identical open-drive Rolls-Royce landaulettes in front of the Tate Gallery, London, 1911. The cars had been ordered by the Government of India for the Delhi Durbar.

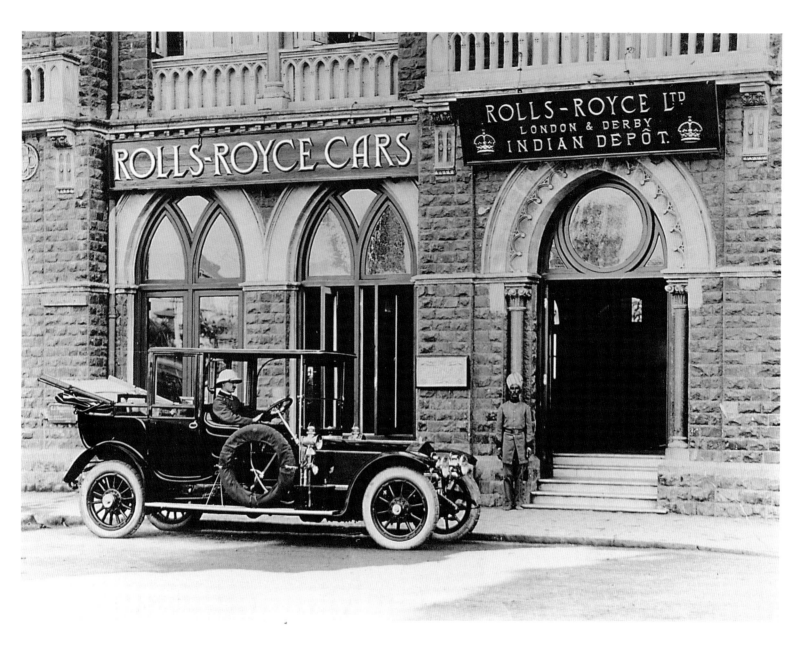

One of the eight Rolls-Royce landaulettes outside the company's India Depot on Mayo Road, Bombay, 1911. In receiving official patronage, Rolls-Royce was firmly established as the pre-eminent automobile in the subcontinent.

ABOVE: A 1957 Mercedes 300 SL belonging to the royal family of Gondal, the forty-fourth car in their fleet.

LEFT: Maharaja Man Singh II and Maharani Gayatri Devi of Jaipur in front of their 1939 Bentley two-door saloon.

FACING PAGE TOP: An American limousine from the fleet of Gaekwar Sayajirao III of Baroda dressed for a flower show, c. 1935.

FACING PAGE BOTTOM: The Swan Car was made by Brooke & Co. in 1910 for Robert Matthewson of Calcutta. Matthewson was so enamoured of the vehicle that he commissioned a smaller model, the Cygnet, which was made for him in India. Both cars were subsequently acquired by Maharaja Ripudaman Singh of Nabha. The picture at left shows Maharaja Hanuwant Singh of Nabha and family in the Swan Car, 1972.

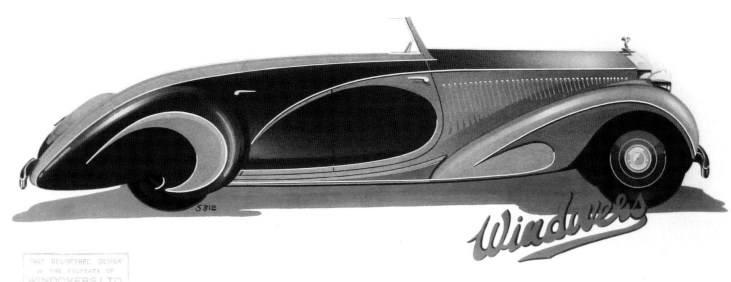

Design for a Windovers Phantom II Tourer, c. 1934-35. This design was translated into a similar car supplied in 1935 to Maharaja Man Singh II of Jaipur. Windovers were established as coachmakers since the late 18th century and with the birth of motor travel began producing car bodies from their premises in Collindale, outside London.

Six-cylinder Delahaye 175 made for Maharaja Jaya
Chamarajendra Wodeyar of Mysore, exhibited in Paris,
1947. The car's interiors were furnished by Hermès.
The Mysore fleet was substantial, containing twenty-four
Rolls-Royces and Bentleys alone.

Windovers Phantom III cabriolet, made for Mir Himayat Ali
Khan, Prince of Berar, 1937.

FACING PAGE: Specifications for Windovers Phantom III cabriolet,
made for Mir Himayat Ali Khan, Prince of Berar, 1937.

283

For: H.H. Prince of Berar   Date of Order 24th June, 1937

Date Chassis received at Works 13th July 1937   Date to be Finished   No. 6283

Type of Body Special cabriolet to design No   Type of Chassis Phantom III R K

5097

SIZE AND PARTICULARS   No.3 CP 116   "E" Steering.

Instrument Board to be finished in dark red bellastoid (mulk finish) Interior
winder & door handle to fold flush into cabinet wax Head lined in dark red
mohair envelope Ivory rim steering wheel Exhaust cut out C.P. centre stop Louvred

Bonnet   Bonnet labs

Interior Seats 4·5 Front seats adjustable one piece, to carry 3 persons. Occasional
seats none   Doors Four   Vents 2 C.P. funnel type on scuttle.

~~Cape Hood~~ Windows Red tinted Triplex in C.P. frames - No lines on

Wind Screen 2 piece V to fold on to the scuttle. Main Triplex glass.

Wings as design V. Special design covered in Staybrite and inset channels.

~~Roof Rail~~ Thermos flask recessed in each rear seat elbow Silver plated sandwich box on o/s main seat.

Luggage ~~Grill~~ Boot flap grid · Tool accom under front seat. No footwells.

~~Lamp Irons~~ Exterior driving mirror · Traffic indicators flush in body side · timed.
Crest large on each spare wheel cover

Painting Front wings, panel top, bonnet and boot in N & H deep cream No 3001
Rear wings, moulding, spare wheel cover & fine lines on discs No H light crimson No·3051

Trimming Gold finish leather, with dark red piping · Head covered in dark red mohair ·
Blinds flap to backlight · blinds to all doors Pullman armrest front & rear ·
Pockets slash type to all doors · Interior Sun Visor · Red silk blind recessed in
top of front seat Front floor dark red leather · Rear carpet dark red pile to tone
with paintwork · Cocktail cabinet behind rear squab lined red baize·

Furniture Int panelling as 5744 job · o/s ashtray, lighter & cigarette box · N/s ashtray & [75 to contain whisky, soda syphon & 3 large glasses·]
lighter · Ashtray & lighter in facia · Untarnishable fittings cubby hole with door & catch·

Electric Light Two interior lights · Rear lights recessed in each wing · Bullet heads Large

~~Footboards, to be covered with~~ recessed wing lamps in nose Spotlights on screen pillars also

Glasses Red tinted Triplex except screen · recessed lamp in spare wheel cover

Number Plates Illuminated built in rear·

Additional Instructions Mounting to R·R print · Private locks in n/s handles, catches o/s·
Two spare wheels · Radio controlled from facia and behind rear squab·
Provision for radiogram in rear boot · Aerial under steps · Detachable spitoon
recessed in o/s of rear seat, to look similar to a speaking tube · Police syren · Musical
Horn & R R horns · Revolver holster each side of dash · Mascot Lalique Flying
Lady with flagstaff attached · Two spare wheel covers · 2 narrow backlights
Triplex · Wide C.P. handles on back of front seat Entrance lights to all doors ·
cubby hole with door & catch · mouldings swaged & Staybrite · Six polished discs
with C.P. rib · C.P. stone guard in front of radiator · Dual electric w/s wipers·
Bumpers special type front & rear as design · Amber centre lamp steering controlled·

Body Completed 23 - 10 · 37   Sent to Paint Loft 12 · 1 · 38

Handed to Mounters 9 - 11 · 37   Delivered 29· 3·38

Car mascot, press-moulded glass. Made by Red Ashay, c. 1930.

FACING PAGE: Car mascot, press-moulded glass. Lalique, c. 1930. Lalique first produced glass mascots in 1925, at which time the firm developed a model of five horses for Citroen's 5CV. It designed a total of twenty-nine stock models. This particular example, called 'Vitesse', was created in 1929 and continued in production until 1947.

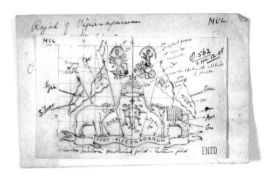
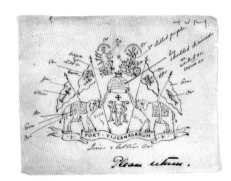

212

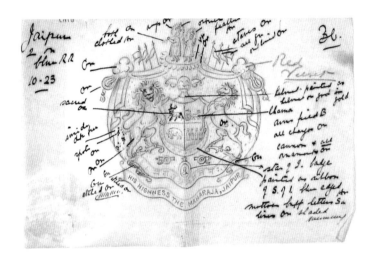

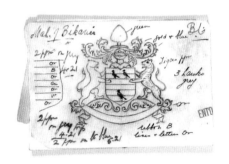

Heraldic designs for Indian princes, ink and pencil on paper: (centre) Jaipur; (clockwise from top left) Vizianagram, Vizianagram, Mysore, Mysore, Rajkot, Rajkot, Bikaner, Udaipur. By H.C. Francis and Geoffrey Francis, early 20th century. It was customary to emblazon prestige vehicles with family arms, a tradition that carried over from the decoration of carriages. These templates belong to an archive of a renowned firm of heraldic artists. In some instances the name of the vehicle is written on the top right hand corner.

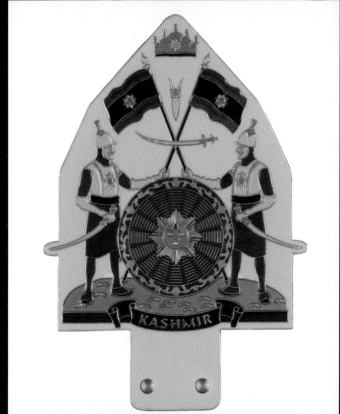

ABOVE LEFT: Design of the coat of arms of Jammu and Kashmir, gouache and ink on paper, early 20th century.

ABOVE RIGHT: Car pennant, brass with enamel. Made for Maharaja Hari Singh of Jammu and Kashmir, c. 1930.

LEFT: Car pennant, brass with enamel. Made for Gaekwar Sayajirao III of Baroda, c. 1930.

As with coaches and palanquins, heraldry was a critical aspect of the decoration of motor cars. Whether applied to the car body or mounted as a pennant, a coat of arms clearly announced the elevated status of the passenger.

FACING PAGE: Rolls-Royce Silver Wraith James Young drop-head coupé, purchased by Maharaja Jaya Chamarajendra of Mysore, 1948. On ascending the throne the prince inherited no fewer than sixty-six cars, to which he added his own purchases, among them this coupé.

DETAILS: Trunk; door with coat of arms; and rear-seat area. The car is finished to a high specification. The fold-out tray is accompanied by silver implements for food and drink while travelling.

Gaekwar Sayajirao III of Baroda in his private railway saloon, early 20th century. With the development of railway in India from the 1850s onwards, princes acquired their own carriages, which could be hooked to mainline services. Private accommodation of this type revolutionised long-distance travel in the subcontinent, making it both easy and comfortable.

217

TOP: Railway saloon made for Gaekwar Sayajirao III of Baroda, 1937.

BOTTOM: Open railway carriage made for Gaekwar Sayajirao III of Baroda, 1937.

Private railway carriages were often constructed in Europe and decorated by leading furnishers such as Waring & Gillow and Maples. Along with motor cars, railway saloons developed into prestige items, and were highly personalised, the exteriors emblazoned with royal coat of arms.

The children of Gaekwar Pratapsinhrao of Baroda, c. 1945.

FACING PAGE: Miniature train. Made by Royal Locomotives for Gaekwar Pratapsinhrao of Baroda, 1943. This miniature railway was given by the ruler to his son Ranjitsinhrao as a present on his fifth birthday. Each morning it transported him and his royal siblings from Laxmi Vilas Palace to the royal school in what is now the Maharaja Fateh Singh Museum.

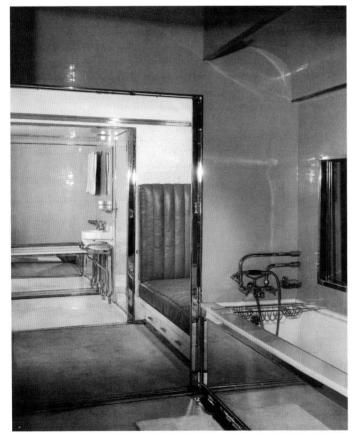

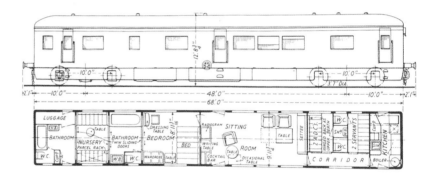

Railway carriage: (clockwise) exterior, elevation and floor plan, bedroom and bathroom. Designed by Eckart Muthesius, 1933 and made by Gloucester Railway Carriage & Wagon Company Ltd., for Maharaja Yeshwant Rao Holkar II of Indore, 1936-37. The carriage was designed with the latest technology and featured air-conditioning, electric utilities, double-glazed windows and mirrored sliding doors. The interior furnishings were provided by Waring & Gillow to the architect's design. Muthesius was also responsible for designing the cutlery, porcelain and bed-linen.

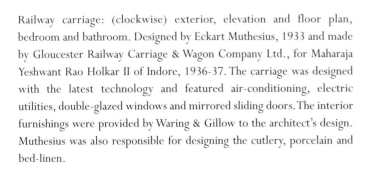

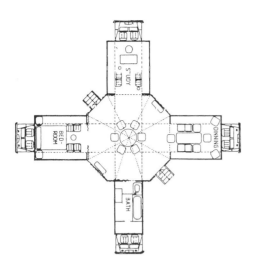

Hunting caravan: (clockwise) floor plan, interior and exterior. Designed by Eckart Muthesius for Maharaja Yeshwant Rao Holkar II of Indore, 1936. The caravan consists of the bodies of four lorries arranged in a cross formation around a central octagonal tented room. Each vehicle served a separate function–as a dining room, bathroom, study and bedroom. The stacking chairs used throughout the tent were produced by PEL–Practical Equipment Limited–a British manufacturer of tubular steel furniture. These photographs were taken by Muthesius himself in the year after the caravan was completed.

224

ABOVE AND BELOW LEFT: Aeroplane and interiors. Made by Airspeed Ltd., the interior designed by Eckart Muthesius for Maharaja Yeshwant Rao Holkar II of Indore, 1937. Airspeed was jointly established by Hesel Tiltman and Nevil Shute Norway, the former acting as chief designer and the latter as chief engineer. In 1951 the firm was acquired by de Haviland.

LEFT: Eckart Muthesius in front of one of the two aeroplanes whose interiors he designed.

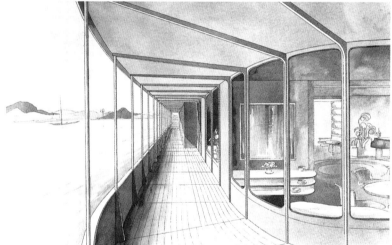

TOP: Model of a houseboat. Designed by Eckart Muthesius for Maharaja Yeshwant Rao Holkar II of Indore, 1934. The boat was conceived as a summer residence for the maharaja for his holidays in Kashmir. Although designed with the latest technical innovations such as air conditioning, the boat itself did not have a motor. The design was never realised.

BOTTOM LEFT: Alternative design for houseboat, configured with a covered walkway, ink and watercolour on paper, c. 1934.

BOTTOM RIGHT: Design for houseboat interior, ink and watercolour on paper, c. 1934.

PALACES

༄

'NOW WE LIVE IN THE NEW PALACE, WHICH IS
CONSIDERED ONE OF THE FINEST IN INDIA. IT
WAS DESIGNED BY A WESTERN ARCHITECT AND
IS BUILT IN AN ECLECTIC STYLE.'

Maharani Sunity Devi,
The Autobiography of an Indian Princess, 1921.

FACING PAGE: Durbar Hall, Jai Vilas Palace, Gwalior. Designed by Sir Michael Filose for Maharaja Jayajirao Scindia, built 1872-74. The carpet for the vast room was woven in the room itself. The chandeliers were supplied by F&C Osler, each holding 248 lights.

Gaekwar Sayajirao III of Baroda, late 19th century.

Laxmi Vilas Palace, Baroda. Designed by Major Charles Mant for Gaekwar Sayajirao III of Baroda, built 1880-90. When Mant died insane the project was taken over by Robert Fellowes Chisholm, a former director of the Madras School of Art. The façade of the palace is a product of High Victorian eclecticism and blends Mughal and Rajput styles with European elements. The hybrid design was conceived to accommodate the latest technologies and the Gaekwar's western lifestyle while simulating the appearance of a traditional Indian palace.

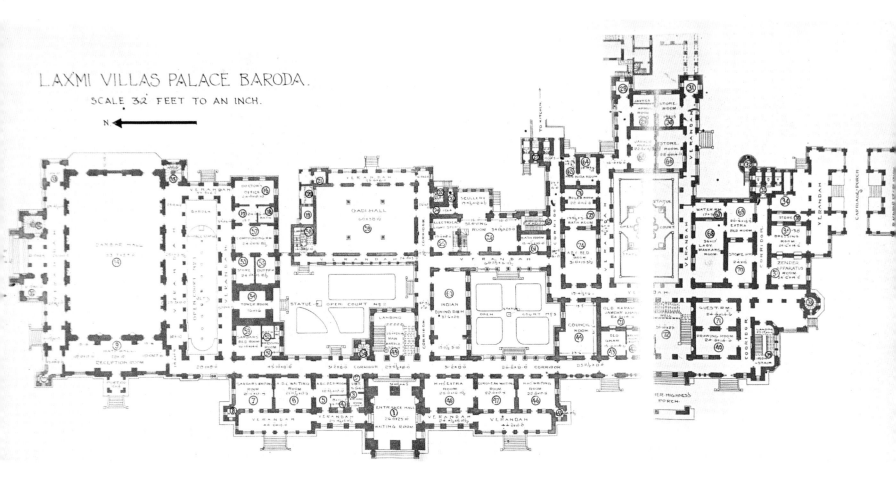

LAXMI VILLAS PALACE BARODA.

SCALE 32 FEET TO AN INCH.

N ←

Laxmi Vilas Palace, built for Gaekwar Sayajirao III of Baroda, 1880-90:

ABOVE: Plan of Laxmi Vilas Palace, c. 1880. The building covers some 100,000 square feet and is divided into three distinct areas: public rooms, the Gaekwar's rooms and the zenana. Although meant to appear like the traditional palace of an Indian prince, Laxmi Vilas was designed with the latest western technical advances in domestic comfort.

LEFT: Gardens, Laxmi Vilas Palace. Designed by William Goldring, c. 1900. The palace grounds were partly laid out as a sculpture park. Formal gardens were planned by Goldring, assistant editor of *The Garden* and President of the Kew Gardens Guild.

FACING PAGE: Letter specifying the costs incurred in the building of Laxmi Vilas Palace, 1957.

No 224
6-5-57

Palace Engineer's Office,
Baroda, dt. 6ᵗʰ May 1957 .

To
The Comptroller of Household,
Khangi Office,
Baroda.

Sub:- Information about the L.V.Palace
Baroda.

Ref:- Your No. 150/23-4-1957.

Sir,

Regarding the above I have to inform you
that the information required about the L.V.Palace is
as under:-

		Year of Cons-truction.	Approxmiate cost of Building.
1.	L.V.Palace main building.	1888-1890	Rs. 59,21,270/-
2.	New Wing Darbar Hall.	1890	Rs. 2,11,954/-
3.	L.V.Palace Kitchen.	1936	Rs. 1,34,234/-
4.	L.V.Palace Main - Entrance Gate.	1923	Rs. 1,70,931/-

The layout of the Garden on the west side
of the L.V.Palace is very appreciable and very handsome.
The view of the west side elevation of the Palace is
artistic and has got architectural beauty.

Yours faithfully,

Superintendent,
Palace Engineer's Office, Baroda.

VMD

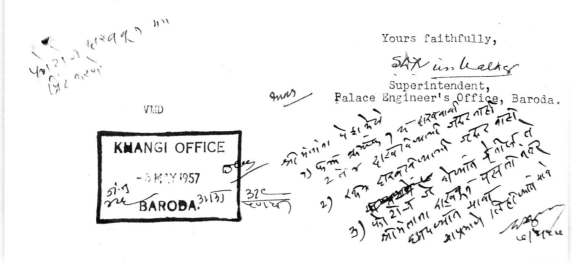

233

235

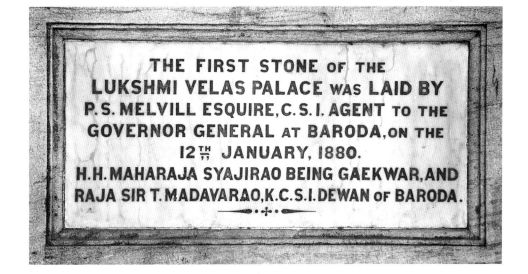

THE FIRST STONE OF THE
LUKSHMI VELAS PALACE WAS LAID BY
P.S. MELVILL ESQUIRE, C.S.I. AGENT TO THE
GOVERNOR GENERAL AT BARODA, ON THE
12TH JANUARY, 1880.
H.H. MAHARAJA SYAJIRAO BEING GAEKWAR, AND
RAJA SIR T. MADAVARAO, K.C.S.I. DEWAN OF BARODA.

Laxmi Vilas Palace, built for Gaekwar Sayajirao III of Baroda, 1880-90:

LEFT: Entrance to the Gaekwar's private apartments, executed in marble imported from Italy and hung with English chandeliers; TOP: Staircase; BOTTOM: Foundation tablet, 1880.

Laxmi Vilas Palace, built for Gaekwar Sayajirao III of Baroda, 1880-90:

The Italian marble table top is inlaid with hardstone portraits of the ruler's second wife, Chimnabai II, and the young Yuvaraj Fatesinhrao, born to Sayajirao from his first wife.

FACING PAGE: Doors to the Durbar Hall are wood with frosted glass bearing the monogram 'GSR'.

240

Design for a palace, pencil and crayon on paper. By Sir
Edwin Lutyens for Maharaja Pratap Singh of Jammu and
Kashmir, 1919. This is one of three designs proposed by
Lutyens for the maharaja, none of which were realised.

LIBRARY AND MUSEUM
RAJA MAHMUDABAD

241

Design for a library and museum, ink and watercolour on paper. By Walter Burley Griffin for Raja Amir Ahmad Khan of Mahmudabad, 1937. Architect of the Australian capital Canberra, Griffin visited India in 1935 and worked in Lucknow before his death almost two years later. This design was proposed by the architect to house the collection of rare books and manuscripts owned by the raja of Mahmudabad, a young prince who shared Griffin's interest in wildlife. The building was never realised; the architect died within days of presenting the raja with the design, which was drawn by his wife, Marion Mahoney.

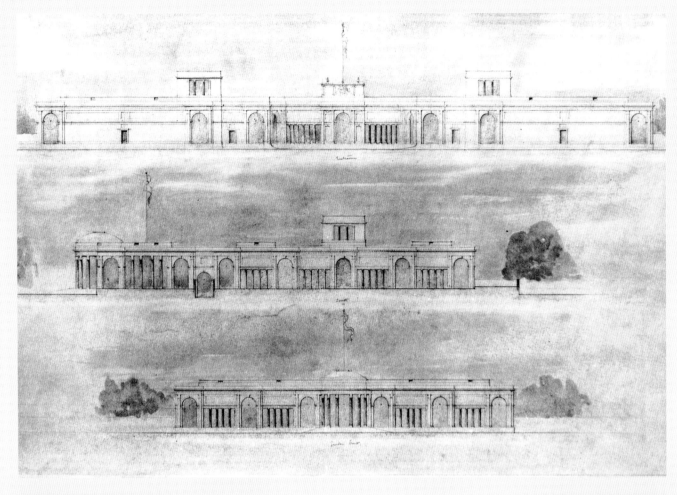

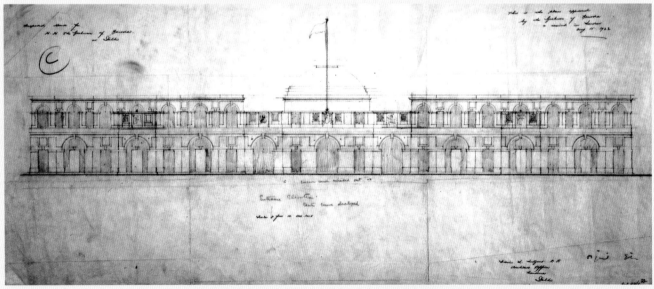

TOP: Design for a palace, pencil and crayon on paper. By the studio of Sir Edwin Lutyens for Maharaja Ganga Singh of Bikaner, 1920. Although this project was never realised, the ruler did erect a palatial residence in Delhi designed by F.B. Blomfield, soon after.

BOTTOM: Elevation and main view of Baroda House, Delhi, pencil, ink and crayon on paper. By Sir Edwin Lutyens for Gaekwar Sayajirao III of Baroda, 1922. Lutyens' work in New Delhi extended to accepting commissions for houses from maharajas who purchased plots in the new capital. Among these was Sayajirao of Baroda, who acquired a site directly on Prince's Park. The classical detailing of Baroda House was designed to harmonise with the overall aesthetic effect of Lutyens' imperial city.

Schemes for a hall and a bedroom, Hyderabad House, Delhi, ink and pencil on paper. By Waring and Gillow for Nizam Osman Ali Khan of Hyderabad, 1932. Lutyens designed Hyderabad House as the grandest princely residence in Delhi, its scale reflecting the rank of the nizam as the senior-most prince in British India. The interiors were decorated by Waring & Gillow in a combination of historic revival and contemporary styles. Interior components such as fibrous plaster, wall panelling, parquetry floors and curtains were all imported from England.

243

Maharaja Umaid Singh of Jodhpur, c. 1940.

Umaid Bhawan Palace, designed by H.V. Lanchester for Maharaja Umaid Singh of Jodhpur, built 1929-44. The vast palace brings together the ancient Hindu architectural concept of a temple-palace with 1930s streamlining. The project itself was partly initiated as an employment exercise in a period of prolonged famine. The architect had considerable training in erecting civic buildings and had been considered for the job of designing New Delhi.

Maharani's Writing Room. The architect designed this room
in tones of silver and gray. The metal secretaire and chair
were designed by Louis Sognot and Charlotte Alix based on
a model that they had exhibited at the Salon D'Automne in
Paris in 1930.

266

Manik Bagh, built for Maharaja Yeshwant Rao Holkar II of Indore, 1930-32:

TOP: Design for the Maharani's Boudoir, watercolour on paper. By Eckart Muthesius, c. 1931.

BOTTOM: Furniture in the Maharani's Boudoir reflects the contemporary taste for East Asian lacquer. Muthesius designed the armchairs and ordered the chaise longue from the Parisian workshop DIM (Décoration Intérieure Moderne).

FACING PAGE TOP: Furniture for the Breakfast Room was designed by Muthesius and produced in Berlin by Johann Eckel. Tableware for the palace was acquired in Paris from Jean Puiforcat.

BOTTOM: The Banqueting Hall table was configured with underlit recesses for flower arrangements. The furniture was designed by Muthesius and produced in Berlin by Johann Eckel. The bronze and nickel silver wall lamps, also by the architect, were made by the Berlin workshop of Max Kruger.

Manik Bagh, built for Maharaja Yeshwant Rao Holkar II of Indore, 1930-32:

ABOVE: Chaise longue, tubular chrome-plated metal. Designed by René Herbst, c. 1931. Herbst was a founding member of the Union des artistes modernes (UAM), a group of designers who promoted simplicity and functionality in their work. Herbst championed tubular metal as the premier material for modern furniture.

LEFT: Design for a carpet, gouache and pencil on paper. By Ivan da Silva Bruhns, 1930. The designer was responsible for carpets for Manik Bagh. The drawing is signed 'da Silva Bruhns, I. Da Silva Bruhns 1930', and '1930-Collection S.A.R.Y.R. Holkar-Maharaja of Indore for recess in private sitting-room N0 647'.

FACING PAGE: Two versions of Bird in Space, marble. By Constantin Brancusi, c. 1933. In addition to these two works, the ruler owned a bronze version of 'Bird in Space', now in the Norton Simon Museum, Pasadena. Although it is unlikely that he received the works until 1936, he seems to have reserved them on a visit to Brancusi's studio in 1933. The two marble sculptures were originally housed in the Banqueting Hall at Manik Bagh, while the bronze was placed in the maharaja's sitting room. Yeshwant Rao asked Brancusi to design an open-air temple to house these works, and although in 1937 the sculptor visited Indore to advance these plans, the project was never realised.

Kapurthala, His Highness The Raja-I-Rajgan Jagatjit Singh of, *My Travels in Europe and America 1893*, London, 1895.

Keith, A. Berriedale, ed., *Speeches and Documents on Indian Policy, 1750-1921*, London, 1922.

Kulkarni, V.B., *Princely India and the Lapse of British Paramountcy*, New Delhi, 1985.

Lathe, A.B., *Memoirs of His Highness Shri Shahu Chhatrapati Maharaja of Kolhapur*, Bombay, 1924.

Llewellyn-Jones, Rosie, *A Fatal Friendship*, Delhi, 1992.

Llewellyn-Jones, Rosie, *A Very Ingenious Man, Claude Martin in Early Colonial India*, Delhi, 1992.

Love, H.D. *Vestiges of Old Madras, 1640-1800*, London, 1913.

Mahtab, B.C. (Maharaja of Burdwan), *Impressions, the Diary of a European Tour*, London, [1908?].

Mahtabsing, Awatsingh, *Something about my Trip to Europe*, Sukkur, 1905.

McClenaghan, Tony, *Indian Princely Medals*, New Delhi, 1996.

Merrick, E.M., *With a Palette in Eastern palaces*, London, 1899.

Metcalfe, Thomas R. *An Imperial Vision*, London and Boston, 1989.

Moore, Lucy, *Maharanis*, New Delhi, 2004.

Nadelhoffer, Hans, *Cartier, Jewellers Extraordinary*, London, 1984.

Nadkarni, Rao Bahadur Ghanasham Nilkanth, *Journal of a Visit to Europe in 1896*, Bombay, 1903.

Natwar-Singh, K., *The Magnificent Maharaja, the Life and Times of Maharaja Bhupinder Singh of Patiala (1898-1931)*, Delhi, 2005.

A Nawab's Dream, exh. cat., Paris: Christofle, 1999.

Niggl, Reto, *Eckart Muthesius 1930, The Maharaja's Palace in Indore, Architecture and Interior*, Stuttgart, 1996.

Nizams' Jewellery, exh. cat., Hyderabad, 2006.

Parks, Fanny, *Wanderings of a Pilgrim in Church of the Picturesque*, London, 1850.

Paul, E. Jaiwant, *The Unforgettable Maharajas*, Delhi, 2003.

Pillai, G. Paramaswaran, *London and Paris through Indian Spectacles*, Madras, 1897.

Prinsep, Val. C., *Imperial India, An Artist's Journals*, 2nd edition, London, 1879.

Prior, Katherine and John Adamson, *Maharajas' Jewels*, Paris, 2000.

Qaisar, Ahsan Jan, *The Indian Response to European Technology and Culture (A.D. 1498-1707)*, Delhi, 1982.

Ragaviah, Pothum Janakummah, ed., *Pictures of England: translated from the Telegu*, Madras, 1876.

Ramusack, Barbara N., *The Indian Princes and their States, The New Cambridge History of India*, III: 6, Cambridge, 2004.

Raulet, Syvlie, *Van Cleef & Arpels*, New York, 1987.

Ray, Man, *Self Portrait*, London, 1963.

Rudolph, Susanne Hoeber, Lloyd Rudolph and Mohan Singh Kanota, eds., *Reversing the Gaze*, Boulder, Colorado, 2002.

Rousselet, Louis, *India and its Native Princes*, revised & edited Lieut-Col. Buckle, London, 1882.

Rudoe, Judy, *Cartier, 1900-1939*, exh. cat., London, 1997.

Russell, W.H., *The Prince of Wales' Tour: A Diary in India*, 2nd ed., London, 1877.

Scindia, Princess Vijayaraje, with Manohar Maglonkar, *The Autobiography of the Dowager Maharani of Gwalior*, London, 1985.

Singh, Bhawani, Raj Rana of Jhalawar, *Travel Pictures: the record of a European tour*, London, 1912.

Singh, Dhananajaya, *The House of Marwar*, New Delhi, 1996.

Singh, Karni, *The Relations of the House of Bikaner with the Central Powers*, New Delhi, 1974.

Tarlo, Emma, *Clothing Matters, Dress and Identity in India*, London, 1996.

Valentia, Viscount George, *Voyages and Travels to India, Ceylon, the Red Sea, Abyssinia, and Egypt in the years 1802-1806*, 4 Vols., London, 1811.

Waghorne, Joanne P., *The Raja's Magic Clothes: re-visioning kingship and divinity in England's India*, University Park, PA, 1984.

Weeden, Rev. Edward St. Clair, *A Year with the Gaekwar of Baroda*, London, 1912.

West, Capt. Edward, ed., *Diary of the Late Rajah of Kolhapoor, during his visit to Europe in 1870*, London, 1872.

Wheeler, J. Talboys, *Madras in the Olden Time*, Madras, 1882.

Whitaker, John, *The Best: a history of H.H. Martyn & Co.*, Cheltenham, 1998.

Wild, Roland, *The Biography of Colonel His Highness Shri Sir Ranjitsinhji*, London 1934.

Wilkinson, Wynyard, *The Makers of Indian Colonial Silver*, London, 1987.

Williams, Elaine, *Maharani, Memoirs of a Rebellious Princess*, Delhi, reprint 2003.

Worlock, George, 'The King of Oudh's Service', *The Spode Review*, Stoke-on-Trent, November 1994.

274

Princess cigarettes, made in Cairo for Maharaja Ganga Singh of Bikaner, 1936. Cigarettes smoked by the ruling family of Bikaner were rolled in paper printed with the state arms. The box reads: 'God save His Highness.'

PHOTO CREDITS

❧